Scotland
A Whisky Lover's
Guide

Ted Bruning

White Mule Press a division of the
American Distilling Institute™.

PO Box 577
Hayward, CA 94543
whitemulepress.com

Copyright © 2016, Ted Bruning

All rights reserved.

ISBN 978-0-9968277-4-4

*Cover photo front—Scapa; back cover—Clynelish at night,
Photo ©Angus Bremner, bremnerphoto.co.uk*

My thanks go to all who have helped with this book, but especially to Rupert Wheeler, without whom it would never have happened at all.

Contents

Part IV
Gin, Vodka, & Rum Distilleries

Appendix I
Speyside

Appendix II
The Whisky Regions of Scotland

Appendix III
Distilleries Closed to the Public

Appendix IV
Distilleries Pending

Map

Foreword

It is a great pleasure to write a foreword to Ted Bruning's *Scotland, A Whisky Lover's Guide*. This book is an excellent, detailed study of the history of distilling in Scotland, the complex procedures involved in moving from barley to the final product, and with succinct descriptions of the principal distilleries.

I would like to establish my credentials to write this piece by pointing out that my own love for whisky, in particular for malt whisky, has had a colossal and dramatic influence on my life. Do not worry; this influence has neither been sordid nor degrading but entirely positive. Indeed, I can safely say that much of my (limited) professional success comes directly from an accident of birth and malt whisky.

I had the great good fortune to be born in Campbeltown, Kintyre, just a stone's throw from the Springbank distillery. Indeed when I smell a glass of Springbank, I immediately think of my mother. My family has lived in the area, with close family connections in Islay, for hundreds of years. It was a strongly West Highland community in which whisky played a central role, a place of noble thinkers, of scholars, and great drinkers. That said, I cannot remember a strong culture of whisky connoisseurship in my early years. People drank blended whisky, in particular "Islay Mist," a blend of Islay malts, reserving malt whisky for special events, such as funerals. There were no grizzled Highlanders sitting around a peat fire mouthing, "Aye, the whisky has a ridge of vanilla leading along mountains of peat, capped with citrus fruits and circled by clouds of sea spray." Such analysis is relatively recent. In the West, back then, whisky was a means to an end.

Things have changed over the last 50 years. Now, to be taken seriously in the worlds of government, finance, and academia, an advanced knowledge of malt whisky is an imperative; accordingly, the importance of Ted Bruning's book.

Let me give you some examples. I went to Washington D.C. to meet the Presidential Science Advisor, we had 5 minutes. I laid my claim for support before him but he was politely disinterested. He then said, "Where are you from? You speak funny." "Scotland." He perks up, "Really, which part?" "Campbeltown, but the family comes from Islay." "You don't say! I am crazy about Islay malts. Hey John, cancel my next meeting. Now Neil, which is the better whisky, Caol

Ila or Ardbeg?" This conversation, more or less word for word, has taken place on many occasions. Starting as strangers, 5 minutes later I have a close friend and we are part of some undefined brotherhood of malt whisky lovers.

In Japan recently, I had a meeting with a university president. It is a very formal affair, with ritualized exchange of business cards. We sit opposite one another across a very large, low table. Conversation is stilted and we both are waiting for the meeting to end. "Where are you from Calder sensei?" "Scotland." I see that light go on. "Ah so, which part of Scotland, Calder sensei?" "Campbeltown, but the family comes from Islay." As is common knowledge, Japanese are good at inscrutability but this information is too powerful. He stands up and bows very low, "I am sorry, but could you tell me if the floor malting at Springbank makes a great difference to the quality of the whisky?" Off we go and it turns out that he has an encyclopedic knowledge of Scottish malts. He also has an astonishing collection of whiskies and before I leave he gives me a 1977 bottle of Ardbeg and a 1980 special Christmas bottle of Glenfarclas. These are the best whiskies I have ever possessed.

There is no doubt that my career has been propelled upwards more due to my place of birth than through ability. I cannot count the number of exchanges similar to the examples above that have taken place in a very wide range of countries. Each time I have made firm friends and I have ruthlessly exploited these friendships for professional advantage.

Understanding whisky is no longer an erudite occupation of a few people sheltering from the rain in Scotland. It is now completely globalized and an essential tool in making friends and influencing people. Look upon Ted Bruning's work as a self-help book.

However it's not just the knowledge of Scottish malt whisky that has become globalized, it is access to the whisky itself. Springbank was always seen as a rare product in Scotland. It was difficult to find and frankly your best bet was to go to Eaglesome's whisky shop in Campbeltown to be sure of getting a bottle.

I now live in Okinawa, a beautiful subtropical island in the middle of the East China Sea. One day I go to a local corner shop that sells seafood, bizarre cuts of pork, and alcohol. Nearly all the booze is Awamori, a rice spirit indigenous to Okinawa, and Sake, but there is also a shelf of whisky. On the shelf there are not only bottles of Springbank, but also bottles of Islay Mist. They are selling for half the price of the same bottles in Scotland. How did they get here?

Perhaps there is a tinge of sadness for me in the modern lack of exclusivity of Scottish malts. It is a bittersweet realization, now that you can buy them anywhere, although no doubt this is a good thing for our proud northern country.

Now here is the rub. These great whiskies evolved from driving rain, the scream of the Herring Gull, rotting creels, holed clinker boats, the cry of the lamb who has lost its mother, the sob of the old woman in the ditch, the stench of rotting seaweed, the grey, the purple, the dark brown.

Can they meaningfully be drunk away from their place of origin?

Recently, knee deep in the turquoise ocean, I was offered a heavily iced glass of Lagavulin. There was wild amaryllis growing on the shore, the smack of the Ruddy Kingfisher as it hit the window, the squeal of children splashing in the sea for fruit, the perfume of plumeria, the screech of the monster fruit bat and the deal clincher: sunshine. I had to refuse the drink.

This book, *Scotland, A Whisky Lover's Guide*, is an excellent survey of the history, distilling practices, and the main sites of whisky culture in Scotland. I learned a great deal by reading it and recommend it to all. It is a book that will gain you access to the global club of whisky aficionados, and almost certainly improve your chances of promotion.

−Neil Calder, 2016. Okinawa, Japan.

Introduction

Top— a peaty burn; Bottom—fresh cut peat on Islay

Scotch is the world's favorite spirit, but to its multitude of fans around the globe it's much more than just a drink. It's liquid history. It's the essence of Highland glen and mountain burn, of loch and of peat-bog, distilled and put in a bottle. And for once, the hyperbole is justified and the romance is reality.

A single malt is just as much the expression of its individual *terroir* as is a château-bottled claret. The peat the malt is dried on, the chemical profile of the water it's mashed in, the shape and size of the vessels the wash is distilled in, the provenance of the oak the new make is matured in—a thousand variables make the character of a single malt what it is. Understandably, therefore, master distillers are deeply averse to change for fear of losing that indefinable yet essential individuality; and their devotion to continuity means that tradition and heritage are not just words but are real, working components in practical everyday use.

This living and functional heritage is an important ingredient in Scotch's appeal to tourists: 10% of Scotland's 15 million annual visitors take a distillery tour as part of their itinerary, and two-thirds of Scotland's malt whisky distilleries now open their doors to the public with facilities ranging from full-blown visitor centers with shops, cafes, and museums to private tours available only by arrangement. And whisky tourism isn't confined to distillery visits: The Malt Whisky Experience in Edinburgh, for instance, is the country's seventh most popular attraction with more 300,000 visitors every year. So whisky is more than just a drink: It's a whole world that you can immerse yourself in.

Before we venture together into the wonderful world of whisky, though, we might as well get a firm grasp of what Scotch actually is. If you're already a keen connoisseur and have visited distilleries before, you will already know much or all of what follows and perhaps even more. But for those readers who are new to the world of peat-smoke and the angel's share, a basic understanding of the materials and processes involved hugely increases the enjoyment you will derive from a distillery tour.

In the rather prosaic terms of the 1988 Scotch Whisky Act, Scotch is the distillate of a fermented wash of malted barley to which whole grains of other cereals may be added, distilled to less than 94.8% alcohol by volume and aged for at least three years in oak casks of 700 liters or more. The only permitted additives are water and caramel; and the end product may not be sold at less than 40% ABV. Finally, the whole process up to blending must be carried out in Scotland.

Dry as dust the legal definition may be, but its legalese conceals the fact that the law seeks to reconcile the two very different spirits of which most whisky is a mixture: malt and grain. Both start life as pretty straightforward beer (minus the hops, of course). But even at this early stage we need to understand the cereals that supply the fermentable material that lies at the heart of any alcohol. So let's start with barley.

A grain of barley is a self-contained package carrying enough carbohydrate to start the growing process. But starch is insoluble, so the grain also contains an enzyme, diastase, which once moistened will convert the starch into sugar (a process called saccharification) that the seedling will live on while it grows its root system. It's this sugar, maltose, that the maltster wants; so the barley is tricked into saccharification by being dunked in warm water, which makes the grain think it's spring and therefore time to sprout. Then as soon as it shows signs of sprouting, and before it can tuck into its store of sugar, the maltster arrests the process by drying it. The fuel used in the drying is critical: modern maltsters blow hot air into great revolving drums full of damp sprouting grain, but historically the choice of fuels was straw, furze, charcoal, coke, or in some lucky localities peat, burning directly under a heap of grain which would be turned from time to time to dry evenly and, hopefully, without scorching. All these fuels produced different flavors, but only peat is still used today because of the distinctive phenolic flavor and aroma its fumes impart to the grain: A very peaty malt such as Laphroaig is either exquisitely smoky or unpleasantly medicinal, depending on your personal taste.

The malted grain is first crushed to the consistency of coarse flour and then steeped in hot water and stirred to dissolve the sugar, just as it would be in a brewery; but instead of being boiled up with hops (as it would be in a brewery), the sweet malt syrup, or "wort," goes directly to what brewers call a "fermenter" and distillers call a "washback," to be pitched with yeast and fermented to 6–9% alcohol by volume. The wash, as the fermented wort is known, is then pumped into the wash still for its first distillation.

A wash still is a bulbous vessel made of or lined with copper (which neutralizes sulphurous compounds), which slightly resembles the domestic copper pot from which it is ultimately descended, but with an inverted funnel on top. The wash in the still is heated to above 78° C (172.4° F), the boiling point of ethanol, originally by direct fire but these days by steam coils, and the vapor that will eventually be Scotch rises into the funnel, or "head." This leads via a pipe called a lyne arm to a condenser, traditionally a coiled copper tube immersed in cold water. Every factor here is a variable. The size and shape of the still, the height and bore of the head, the length of the lyne arm and even the angle at which it's set all influence the separation of unwanted compounds such as aldehydes, methanol, and fusel oil from the pure ethanol.

Malt whisky is distilled twice or even three times. The first pass separates out the undesirable compounds, the resulting liquid being called "low wines." The low wines flow through the spirit safe, which is a locked glass box that allows the stillman to discard the first and last runnings—the foreshots and feints—which can be recycled and redistilled later on. The acceptable portion, or middle cut, which is generally around 25% ABV, then goes to the spirit still, which is usually a little smaller than the wash still, for the process to be repeated. Once again the first and last runnings are discarded and recycled, while the middle cut—the raw and fiery "new make"—goes to the spirit receiver to be filled into oak casks.

Here it's not only the length of maturation but also the barrel itself that counts. The oak leaches tannin, which colors the spirit, and vanillin, which smooths it. A little of the ethanol—the "angels' share"—evaporates through the porous staves, softening the palate. Any residual fusel oils, aldehydes and congeners will break down over time. The new make also absorbs flavors from the barrel's previous occupant. American distillers use their casks only once, and many of the discards are exported to Scotland; the insides of Bourbon casks are charred before filling and therefore have a particular character. Sherry casks are often used to "finish" maturing stocks—that is, mature whisky is filled into them for the last few months before bottling. As the whisky industry becomes more and more experimental, casks of many other provenances and backgrounds—rum, brandy, even wine—are also being pressed into service to create new and distinctive expressions.

That, in very simplified terms, is how malt whisky makes its way from field to bottle. But less than half of the whisky we drink is made this way. Grain whisky, of which our everyday blended whiskies are mainly composed, is very different. For a start, the wash can be composed of only 20% malted barley and 80% other, cheaper, grains—chiefly maize (corn) or rye. They don't even have to be malted. The low malt content supplies enough diastase to saccharify all the rest.

Another difference, and perhaps the most striking, is the equipment used to distil grain whisky. The patent or continuous or column still is essentially a loop formed of two connected upright columns into which wash and steam flow continually in opposite directions, the wash descending and the steam rising. First the hot steam evaporates the ambient-temperature wash; then the fresh wash pouring in at ambient temperature condenses the alcoholic vapor. The various constituents of this vapor, though, all condense at different temperatures and so liquefy on their own bubble-plates in one of the columns, to be collected separately. Thus freed from the less desirable compounds, the ethanol continues its rise to the top of the column to be condensed and collected at 90% or more purity.

But can this really be called whisky? In 1905 a London borough decided that it couldn't, and summonsed a publican for selling blended Scotch, arguing that the spirit produced from mixed grain via a continuous still was so different from that of barley malt and pot-still that it could hardly use the same name. The publican was convicted. The whisky industry promptly exercised its nascent but already considerable muscle to lobby for and, in 1908, to get a Royal Commission which eventually declared that if it was made in Scotland, and so long as the grist, of whatever grain, was saccharified by the diastase of malt, that would do. And to be fair, if you ever get a chance to blind-taste a well-matured single grain such as Cameron Brig against a light single malt, there's a good chance that you won't be able to tell which is which.

In contrast to the Cognac industry, where the blender is king and single-estate, single vintage bottlings are a comparative novelty, a single malt is generally considered the acme of Scotch whisky. Few of us, though, are wealthy enough to be able to make single malts our regular tipple, so instead we look for a blend with as much refinement and sophistication as our budgets will run to. The price and quality of a blended whisky depend on a number of variables: The character of the malts; the proportion of malt to grain; the age of both (where an age is stated, it will be that of the youngest whisky in it). But a blend need not always be your second choice: A high-malt blend including a soupcon or more from some rare and ancient vat may be finer and more expensive than a basic single malt.

Whatever your dram of choice, though, the pleasure you take from it can only be enhanced by a visit to its place of birth.

PART ONE

The Story of Scotch

Sean Gordon of Bruichladdich, photo ©Anton Sucksdorff Photography

Distilling, or separating mixed substances by temperature management, is the oldest industrial technology of all. In prehistory distillation was used to extract metals from their ore and also to separate salt from brine; but it was not until the 8th and 9th centuries CE that Arab chemists discovered how to condense ethanol from vaporized wine. The teetotal Muslims used their ethanol as a solvent capable of extracting alkaloids—that is, the active constituents, which are not water-soluble—from medicinal herbs; hence its name in many languages: *ma'ul-hayat, aqua vitae, usquebaugh...* water of life.

This discovery, like many others of the Islamic Enlightenment, soon reached the great medical school in Salerno and was carried all over Christendom by the monks who studied there. But until the late middle ages distillation remained the province mainly of the monastic infirmarer. In northern Europe particularly, the base material, wine, was simply too expensive to be distilled in anything but small quantities; and it wasn't until the 15th century that it was discovered—simultaneously in many countries, it seems—that ale could be distilled too.

Whisky's birth year is generally taken to be 1495, when the Scottish Exchequer Roll records the grant of eight bolls of malt to Friar John Cor from which to make aqua vitae; and although precise dates are hotly disputed, this is more or less contemporary with the first distillations of other grain-based spirits including vodka and schnapps.

At that stage, spirits were still mainly produced as expensive matrices for herbal medicines, to be sparingly dispensed in monastic infirmaries. This changed once the monks' monopoly was broken: Unlike the miserly infirmarer, the apothecary wanted to sell as much medicine as he could and dilute it as much as he could. But it was still medicine: Even early vodka was herbal; and as late as 1755 Dr. Johnson defined "usquebaugh" as being "drawn over aromaticks"—so, more like gin than modern whisky.

For the genesis of whisky as we know it we have to look beyond medical science and into the countryside, where distilling proved a boon to farmers. It was easy enough: The only equipment necessary was the wash-copper, a coil of copper tubing, and a tub of cold water. And it meant that in good years farmers no longer had to sell their surplus at glut prices but could distill it and store it in oak casks almost indefinitely against the lean years to come. As we have seen, it was the chemical changes brought about by storage in oak that transformed neutral white spirit into whisky—and the longer it was stored, the better it became.

In 1725 rioting followed an increase in the malt tax introduced from England, and 11 Glaswegians were shot dead by dragoons.

By the late 16th century, distilling had become so widespread in Scotland that in 1579 it had to be suspended for a year following a failed harvest. Records are patchy though, because whisky wasn't taxed and therefore didn't figure in official accounts. Only in 1644, when Scotland joined the war that had been raging in England for nearly two years, were spirits taxed. Taxation seems not to have been contentious though, until after the union of England and Scotland in 1707: In 1725 rioting followed an increase in the malt tax introduced from England, and 11 Glaswegians were shot dead by dragoons. However those rioters were townsfolk not countrymen, and consumers rather than distillers; for at this early stage the small distillers were neither organized racketeers nor armed gangs like smugglers in England. Eventually, illicit or "bothie" distilling became a full-time occupation for many; but in the early 18th century the distillers were still by and large ordinary tenant farmers who only wanted to carry on as their forefathers had, and who had the support of consumers. They also had the ambivalent support of their landlords.

After many years of war the lairds needed to revive the fortunes of their rugged and unruly estates, but faced a dilemma. On the one hand they wanted legitimate, duty-paying distillers to flourish, and would have loved to suppress their tenants' untaxed enterprises; on the other, the same tenants paid their rents with the income from illegal distilling. Over the years, though, the lairds' uneasy complacence hardened. In the early 18th century the Highlands were still almost feudal; but the failure of the 1745 uprising made the fealty of an armed and warlike tenantry redundant and left the lairds with overpopulated and unproductive estates. They therefore began to reform in much the same way that English landowners were doing. As "improving" landlords they appeared to be very progressive, founding a great number of well-planned and well-built new towns such as Oban, Grantown-on-Spey, Elgin, Keith, and Tobermory to improve conditions for their tenants. But the purpose of their founders was hardly altruistic: The new urban plantations were a conscious and deliberate device to cleanse the Highlands of their surplus population and make way for livestock.

Legal distilleries were common features of the new towns, intended to find employment for the tenants and income for landlords, but despite the efforts of insufficient and corruptible excise officers or gaugers, they were so effectively undercut by the bothie distillers that many went out of business. But conditions in the Highlands were changing inexorably in favor of the lairds. The job of cleansing by urbanization was followed by near-genocidal forced clearances between 1790 and 1820, when crofts were simply burnt down and their inhabitants evicted wholesale. Less labor-intensive cattle and sheep replaced the arable; and the social pattern that ensured a smuggler could either trust or intimidate his neighbors was disrupted by urbanization. Not that there was no secret distilling in towns; but with potential informers only the thickness of a party wall away, it was a risky business.

By 1823 the landowners had established sufficient control over their estates to be able to promise that, with a little latitude, they could suppress illegal distilling almost entirely; and that year's Excise Act set out new, more lenient regulations that made it possible to distil on a small scale both legally and profitably. It was a watershed in the history of Scotch. On its eve there were 111 licensed stills in Scotland; three years later there were 263. In the same period, Britain's legal spirits production doubled to just over 18 million proof gallons, or 80 million liters of pure alcohol. Such a dramatic increase in legal production demonstrates not only the scale of illicit distilling but also the desire of illicit distillers to get on the law's right side.

But although whisky was now respectable, finding a market for what was, outside Scotland, a novelty, was not easy. The first hurdle the distillers faced was the variability of their product.

Highland whisky was reputedly all-malt; but other grains and other fermentables were often used to pad it out. The malting process itself could be crude: Sacks of barley were soaked in bog-water, allowed to sprout, and then unevenly parched over wood or peat fires. There are also records of small distillers continuing to use botanicals more generally associated with gin, especially herbs and wildflowers, but on occasion juniper berries and orange peel. Hurried distillation meant that some Highland products were high in heavy alcohols, especially fusel oil, and maturation was haphazard. The breadth of the spectrum, ranging from fresh, pale, and aromatic to dark, viscous, and vinous must have been utterly confusing to unfamiliar consumers.

The column still, perfected in Dublin by Aeneas Coffey in 1830, eventually provided the answer. Producing a continuous stream of very pure ethanol from a grain bill of only 20% malted barley and 80% unmalted cereals, it was the perfect device for the mass production of raw spirit for rectification; but it also became the essential piece of technology in Scotch whisky's battle for a mass market. Pioneering merchants such as Arthur Bell of Perth and Andrew Usher of Edinburgh who understood the importance of consistency first started blending different whiskies from the distilleries they represented to produce a degree of uniformity and a brand identity that drinkers could recognize. Neutral spirit from continuous stills allowed them to smooth out any jarring or overpowering notes. The admixture of the much cheaper grain spirit also brought the price within the reach of the common man.

Adulteration by wholesalers and retailers was another hurdle. Like most commodities whisky was shipped in casks, which made it vulnerable to tampering. The merchant might make three barrels out of two; the grocer or publican might buy two and make another three. Additives used to disguise the watering down ranged from the harmless—cheap sherry, tea, glycerine, fruit concentrates—to the lethal—meths, turpentine, even sulfuric acid. A famous attempt to expose adulteration in 1872 came to nothing: The North British Daily Mail hired a chemist to analyze more than 30 samples bought at random from Glasgow pubs. Many were entirely synthetic and contained no whisky whatever. The revelation provoked debate but no action. Proprietary bottling was the blenders' response to adulteration, but by creating an affordable small package and allowing the creation of an eye-catching brand the consumer could trust, it also proved final step in creating a mass-market product.

These innovations heralded a 40-year golden age which started in earnest in 1862, when a tiny but voracious aphid arrived in France from North America to wean the English off their brandy. Within a very few years Phylloxera had destroyed 40–50% of France's vineyards. In the 1870s the French began replanting with American rootstock, which was immune, but the vineyards of Cognac would take more than a decade to recover. By the mid-1870s brandy was in short supply. Scotch wasn't.

The speed and scale of Scotch's advance created the danger of running out of the malts the blenders needed, and their response was to start buying and extending existing distilleries.

This must have been one of the greatest opportunities for a nascent industry in the history of commerce, and the whisky merchants were not slow to exploit it by establishing agencies first in London, then throughout the British Empire and the capital cities of the world. The speed and scale of Scotch's advance created the danger of running out of the malts the blenders needed, and their response was to start buying and extending existing distilleries, and building new ones by the dozen. In 1885–87 the journalist Alfred Barnard toured all 129 working Scottish distilleries; had he made the same tour in 1900 he would have had to visit 30 more. The architect Charles Doig, designer of the "pagoda" maltings so emblematic of the Scottish distillery, was alone responsible for building or rebuilding 56 of them.

Then in 1898, Pattison Brothers, a Leith whisky merchant that had expanded hugely and entirely on credit, went bust owing huge sums to its suppliers. The aftershocks forced the closure of 60 distilleries and left the industry holding enough stock to slake a third of Britain's annual demand. Nevertheless the industry as a whole was solid: Demand was strong and the trade was profitable.

The chaos, though, provided the ideal springboard for a new breed of conglomerate.

The first and biggest, the Distillers Company Ltd. or DCL, originated in 1856 when the largest grain distillers formed a cartel to fix prices and carve up the market. In response, the other grain distillers formed the rival North British Distillery Company, but DCL was always the stronger and on the collapse of Pattison Brothers was able to buy their Leith warehouses, newly built at a cost of £60,000, for just £25,000. It and the other big blenders also spent the first decade of the new century consolidating, mainly through financial restructuring and the development of marketing and advertising campaigns. How far they had succeeded was about to be put to the sternest possible test.

...big blenders...spent the first decade of the new century consolidating, mainly through financial restructuring and the development of marketing and advertising campaigns.

When World War I broke out, privations were only to be expected; but nobody anticipated how great they would be. It was just the industry's luck that Lloyd George, Chancellor when the Great War erupted, was a fanatical teetotaller who considered drink a more dangerous enemy than the Germans and was seriously considering complete prohibition. The industry bought breathing space by converting grain distilleries to acetone and industrial alcohol production; but output of malt whisky was halved while duty was doubled. One by one the malt distilleries closed, leaving the blenders anxious as to where their fillings were to come from. As in the 1890s, they started buying capacity.

When peace came, demand was held back by further increases in duty; by the popularity of gin among younger drinkers; by the economic woes of the times; and, of course, by Prohibition in the USA. The 133 working distilleries of 1920 fell to a mere 15 by 1933. Most of the silent stills were not dead, of course, but sleeping: Distillery equipment could be mothballed with little maintenance; and the remote locations of many distilleries, together with their specialized nature, made them difficult to sell for other purposes, especially in a depression. Nonetheless, the independent sector was all but wiped out between 1925 and 1933, with only the hardier companies such as William Grant, Highland Distillers, and Glenfarclas clinging on.

DCL, though, was easily big and strong enough to catch the more desirable malt distilleries as they fell, acquiring Glendullan, Glenlossie, Caol Isla, Clynelish, Old Pulteney, and Balmenach. It could also mop up its major competitors: Haig & Haig, John Haig, Scottish Malt Distillers and Buchanan-Dewar's, Johnnie Walker, and White Horse Distillers between 1922 and 1927. DCL wasn't the only predator, though. From the moment Prohibition came into force, mobsters started running Scotch from Canada into the US across the Detroit River separating Windsor, Ontario, from Detroit. The Detroit Purple Gang and the Little Jewish Navy bought their stock from a legitimate businessman, Samuel Bronfman of Seagram Distillers of Windsor. Bronfman sensed that once Prohibition was over, whoever had footholds in both Scotland and the US would make a killing. The same idea had occurred to another legitimate Windsor distiller, Hiram Walker, which bought Glenburgie-Glenlivet in 1930 and Ballantine's in 1936, and built the Inverleven grain distillery in 1938.

The 1930s were kind to the industry. The world economy started recovering, for one thing. President Roosevelt took office on 20 January 1933 and quickly repealed Prohibition, while his reflationary New Deal created demand in the US. Rearmament in Britain from 1934 on generated jobs, disposable income, and demand for luxuries. Many distilleries came out of mothballs, and the number at work rose from 1933's low point to 92 at the outbreak of World War II.

When rationing was introduced in January 1940, Scotch wasn't included. But the government closed the grain distilleries and slashed the allocation of barley for malting, and by 1944 there was only one distillery working; sharp rises in duty crippled home demand, and most of wartime production was exchanged for dollars. When the SS Politician of Whisky Galore fame sank in 1941 she was carrying 28,000 cases of Scotch, or a third of a million bottles, all destined for the US.

Churchill, though, was no Lloyd George: He understood the value of the whisky industry. So did the post-war Labour Government: It gradually increased the industry's grain allocation, but deterred home consumption with yet more duty increases. Not until 1953 was wartime regulation abolished altogether, but by then the mothballed distilleries were already back at work earning dollars. In 1945, 56 distilleries reopened, and by 1950 the number working had reached 95—more than in 1939.

In the same year, foreign investors returned when Seagram's bought Strathisla, and in 1954–1955 Hiram Walker bought Glencadam, Scapa, and Pulteney. In 1956 Schenley Industries of New York bought Long John, the Glenugie malt distillery, and the Strathclyde grain distillery complex inside which it built a new malt distillery. It also built Tormore in Speyside in 1958. The following year another American-backed investor, Inver House, built both a grain and a malt distillery, Glenflagler near Airdrie.

By 1961 production had returned to pre-war levels and exports were taking off—£81 million in 1962, £872 million in 1982. To cope with predicted demand, which in the whisky industry has to be estimated several years ahead, more than a dozen new distilleries sprang up in the 1960s and 1970s, some of them—Isle of Jura, Glenallachie, Tamnavulin—destined to become highly-praised single malts in their own right.

The scale of expansion and Scotch whisky's increasingly international appeal inevitably attracted yet more global investors: Pernod-Ricard, Martini-Rossi, Remy-Cointreau. British brewers were big investors too: Scottish & Newcastle bought McKinlay's in 1960, opening Isle of Jura in 1963 and Glenallachie in 1968; Courage, Watney, Whitbread and Allied also bought into the industry, acquiring both merchants and distilleries. The economic downturn of the early 1980s found the industry not only overendowed with capacity but also carrying a huge surplus of stock. DCL was particularly exposed: Between 1982 and 1985, 21 of its distilleries were either mothballed or closed for good. It was an outward sign of inner weakness, and in 1986 Guinness, owner of Perth distiller and blender Arthur Bell, took over DCL itself after a titanic battle and amid much controversy, becoming the world's biggest spirits company. Allied, too, was on the hunt: In 1984 it bought both United

Rum Merchants and Hiram Walker, and in 1989 it acquired Whitbread's spirits business including Laphroaig, the famously peaty Islay malt distillery.

The dominance of the Scotch whisky industry by British brewers did not last. Their monopolistic tendencies triggered new regulations that sparked a corporate meltdown in which the brewers frantically reshuffled assets that by now included well over half of the Scotch whisky industry. The biggest beneficiaries were the two supergroups that eventually arose from the chaos: Pernod Ricard and Diageo. Pernod Ricard today includes the empire that was created in 1994 when Allied merged with Spanish wines and spirits giant Pedro Domecq to create Allied Domecq. Diageo was born out of Guinness's long chain of mergers and acquisitions and owns half the distilleries in Scotland and the world's leading blend in Johnnie Walker.

The creation of these two giants led to the appearance of a number of smaller but still formidable conglomerates, mostly formed of distilleries discarded by Diageo and Pernod Ricard to satisfy the competition authorities. They include Inver House, which is owned by a Thai company, International Beverage Holdings; Burn Stewart, bought by Distell of South Africa in 2013; Whyte & Mackay, bought by United Breweries of India in 2007; John Dewar, owned by Bacardi; Morrison Bowmore, bought by Suntory in 1994; and Glenmorangie, part of the French LVMH luxury goods group. Four other malt distilleries are individually owned by foreign investors; 29 are independently or family owned, the biggest concerns being William Grant and the Edrington Group.

So, from its humble beginnings as a by-product of small-scale crafting, Scotch whisky has become a globally traded commodity, with export sales worth over £4 billion in 2012 and BRIC markets catching up with North America, Japan, and Europe. This success has prompted the big firms to build giant new distilleries such as Ailsa Bay and Roseisle to make sure they have fillings to satisfy future demand; but it has also prompted the re-emergence of a craft sector with ambitions to revive the values and techniques of an era long past.

PART TWO
Craft Comes to Scotland

Loch Ewe Distillery

*T*hirty years ago the distilling industry in Britain seemed ossified: Nothing had happened for years, and given the conditions of the times, nothing seemed likely to happen either.

Yet it was a time of terrific energy and dynamism in the UK's microbrewing sector, now in its second decade, and beginning to discover its true potential as consumer demand grew and the retail trade started to open up. The same energy extended, if to a lesser extent, to artisanal cider and wine making. But there seemed no appetite among small independent drinks industry entrepreneurs to establish craft distilleries.

In Scotland, continual contraction and expansion is as normal and as slow as the rhythmic rise and fall of a recumbent elephant's flank as the market goes through its long cycle of demand and supply. Distilleries open and close as often as the executives whose job it is to predict demand think right: Tormore, Macduff, Deanston, Glenallachie, Tomintoul, Tamnavulin, Mannochmore, Braeval, Auchroisk, and Allt a Bhaine all belong to the 15 years 1960–1975, when a number of grain distilleries were built as well.

South of the border, the situation was very different. Between the end of World War II and 1984 only five new licenses to distil were issued in England and Wales. One of them, in 1955, allowed the reopening of the tiny Langley Green gin distillery in Birmingham after its long wartime slumber. The other four issues all stemmed from the trend towards concentration and rationalization that characterized so many British industries during their post-war vicissitudes, and record the moves of many old-established London gin distillers from expensive, cramped, and awkward inner-city sites to more spacious homes further out. In the late 1950s and early 1960s Booth's moved from Turnmill Street to a larger building in Clerkenwell Road; James Burroughs moved from Lambeth to Kennington; and Gilbey's moved even further, from Camden Town to Harlow in Essex. Then in 1984 Gordon's moved from Clerkenwell to Laindon, also in Essex, taking Booth's and Tanqueray, formerly of Finsbury, along with it. In the same period many once-familiar London distillery names also either moved into these great gin factories or vanished entirely: Curtis of Stepney, Seager of Deptford, Nicholson's of Clerkenwell, Langdale's, also of Clerkenwell. Of all

To start a revolution...you need two things: A dissatisfied populace, or...a madman...

the once-great London distillers only Burroughs now remained in its native city.

Identical stories could be told of many other industries in which pre-war Britain had led the world: Motor manufacture, aerospace, electronics—one by one, and often with a hefty shove from the government of the day, they merged, were sold abroad, or were nationalized. In this atmosphere, and given these trends, any sort of innovative thinking in industry was hard enough. In the distilling industry in particular, the general negativity of the times was compounded by an implied moral disapproval of spirits and a severe regulatory regime, both rooted in the conflicts of the 18th century—coastal smuggling, London's gin fever, Scottish moonshining. To make matters worse, excise duty was set extremely high; spirits were therefore priced as luxury goods with a commensurately limited appeal; to invest in any sort of brand-new distillery would be folly. So entrenched was this attitude that it would take a near-revolution to overcome it.

To start a revolution—and it doesn't matter what sort of revolution you plan to start—you need two things: A dissatisfied populace, or at least a public open to new ideas, and a madman, or at least a stubborn and charismatic entrepreneur because, as George Bernard Shaw remarked, "all progress depends on the unreasonable man."

By the mid 1980s the public had certainly proved itself open to new ideas. The traditional big sellers—whisky, gin, dark rum—had been losing share in the home market for 20 years. The major corporations had very firmly prioritized the bulk sellers—big-name gins and standard blended whiskies—to generate the domestic revenues that would allow them to invest in burgeoning export markets. These were almost all mature brands, in many cases approaching their centenaries; their quality and their tradition were rather taken for granted and there was little or nothing in the way of innovation to make them appealing to new consumers. Much as traditional British ales were losing ground to Continental-style lagers, gin, whisky, and dark rum were being eclipsed among younger drinkers by the easier-drinking and very mixable vodka and, to a lesser extent, white rum.

Shaw's "unreasonable man" appeared in 1982, and in a completely different place from where you might have expected. You might have expected that a man who had convinced himself that there was a compelling case for starting up a genuinely new distillery and that the idea was capable of being realized would be a Scot—someone with some knowledge of the subject, working in an environment where the proposal did not seem so egregious. And in fact a Glasgow whisky-broker, George Christie, had been working on building a malt distillery on the site of an old mill at the end of a farm track in deepest Inverness-shire for 20 years. But his plans were nowhere near complete, and unlikely as it seems now—and seemed then—it was a Hereford man who became the first in the new wave of craft distillers.

Bertram "Bertie" Bulmer had recently retired as chairman of the world's biggest cidermaker and was still full of vim and vigor. In 1981 he was instrumental in founding the Hereford Cider Museum, and shortly afterwards acquired an antique Norman *alembic ambulant* which, like him, dated back to 1902 and which he decided to install in the museum. Not for any sound reason (distilling having died out in the region at least 140 years before), but because he wanted to. The story of his two-year struggle to get Customs to issue him a license to distil, and the even longer battle to get the European authorities to permit his product to be designated as cider brandy (according to the European Union, brandy is made of grapes), belongs elsewhere. Suffice to say that he won, and that production of King Offa Cider Brandy continued until 2010, when it was suspended because it was interfering with the museum's main business of being a museum.

Precisely the same battles, but even more grueling and protracted, faced the next unreasonable man into the arena: Julian Temperley, the doyen of the craft distilling movement since Bertie Bulmer's death in 1993. Temperley, owner of Pass Vale Farm at Burrow Hill in Somerset, first set up his Somerset Cider Brandy Company in the outbuildings at the county's finest country house, Brympton D'Evercy Hall, home (then)

[Bertram "Bertie" Bulmer] a Hereford man...became the first in the new wave of craft distillers.

> Malt whisky is the spirit not only of the malt of which it's made, but also of the place where it's made.

of the wonderfully named Clive-Ponsonby-Fane family. After four years of wrangling with customs, the first spirit trickled from the company's still—like Bertie Bulmer's, an antique French pot-still—in 1987. Two years later the enterprise stepped up a gear, moving to Pass Vale Farm itself and re-equipping with two column stills, Fifi and Josephine. It instantly won huge attention and plaudits from the foodie media and is still going strong. Temperley has also helped other cider producers, perhaps most notably the monks of Ampleforth Abbey, distil their products.

Bulmer and Temperley didn't start a revolution, though, and more than a decade was to pass before an imitator appeared on the English and Welsh scene. The two men were classed, unfairly, as "characters," which is a very English and very patronizing euphemism for eccentrics to be admired but not emulated; and their products were for a long time, and equally unfairly, regarded as imitation Calvados. Even their triumphs over bureaucratic adversity were considered, while laudable, to be awful warnings of what the founder of a new distillery might expect to have to suffer. In the years that followed, therefore, there was a mere trickle of openings: Only three in the 1990s, in fact, and two of those in Scotland. George Christie's Speyside distillery finally came on stream in 1990 having been built entirely by hand by a local drystone waller, to be followed five years later by Isle of Arran, brainchild of another senior whisky executive, Harold Currie. (The decade's third foundation, Thames Distillers in Clapham, South London, lies well outside the scope of our current enquiry).

This was a time when the major distilling conglomerates were actually mothballing surplus capacity; but Currie—just retired from the board of Chivas Brothers—had a different vision of the future. Malt whisky is the spirit not only of the malt of which it's made, but also of the place where it's made. Lochranza on Arran, the nearly round island cradled between the Ayrshire coast and the Mull of Kintyre, was chosen as the place because of its history of illicit whisky-making, with frequent armed clashes between excisemen and smugglers; because of the quality of its water; and because of the beauty of its setting and the tourists that it attracted. For, somewhat unusually for the times, Currie earnestly wanted to draw people to the place and a visitor center was always part of the plan. An impromptu flypast by a pair of golden eagles at the official opening was interpreted as a sign of the island's blessing upon the venture.

Remarkable and pioneering though the openings of Speyside and Arran were, it's questionable how deeply they influenced or inspired the craft distillers who came after them a decade later. Currie and Christie have not really been seen as representative of the craft distilling movement that came in their wake—not, at least, by the craft distillers themselves. They were very mainstream, true—not just experienced executives with long careers in the whisky industry behind them, but very senior executives at that. Hardly rebels, then. And while more than half of the first-generation British microbrewers were refugees from the mainstream industry, suit-and-tie men made redundant in the tsunami of brewery closures that swept Britain in the 1960s and 1970s and equipped with redundancy checks, the profits of downsizing, a lot of technical expertise, and in most cases a great deal of business acumen, in Scotland few of the post-1995 new wave distillers had previously been industry insiders. Quite the contrary, in fact: Many craft distillers, particularly if they're in the gin business, would identify themselves (or are identified by their admirers) as urban, cosmopolitan, hip, experimental, free-spirited, rebellious, idealistic, countercultural. Some of them even live up to the billing. The first two of Scotland's independent distillers, however, didn't.

Just 24 hours separated the first flow of new make from the spirit stills at Kilchoman, on Islay's surprisingly sandy Atlantic shore, on 14th December 2005, and at Daftmill at Cupar near Fife on the far side of the country the following day. Both distilleries are on farms and both Anthony Wills at Kilchoman and Francis and Ian Cuthbert at Daftmill had set out to make the best use of their own resources of spring wa-

> Many craft distillers...would identify themselves... as urban, cosmopolitan, hip, experimental, free-spirited, rebellious, idealistic, countercultural.

ter and barley in the same way that Scottish farmers routinely did in the 16th and 17th centuries. But venturing into distilling was a decision that looked forward as well as backward. Backward to the days when, rather than having to dump the surplus barley of a good harvest on the market at glut prices, Scottish farmers maintained its value by distilling it and storing it against the lean times (and it was this storage in oak that transformed neutral spirit into whisky); forward to the economic necessity for Western farmers to add value to their produce by processing it themselves, thereby defending themselves against being undercut by cheap imports.

Although Wills and the Cuthbert brothers were the first actually to fill their new make into oak, others had been working on their own plans at the same time and had only narrowly been pipped at the post, and 2006 saw two more openings that go to show how diverse the appeal of distilling was. For Strathleven on its industrial estate in Dumbarton and Loch Ewe in the near-uninhabited wilderness of Wester Ross were very different types of operation.

Strathleven was established by a partnership that includes Ricky Christie, son of the founder of Speyside and previously its managing director. Their aim, from first firing up their custom-made copper pot still on 13th April 2006, was to produce the purest possible spirits—not just whisky, but gin and vodka as well—entirely from Scottish malt. This goes right back to John Cor and his contemporaries across Northern Europe, who distilled malt liquor to produce a neutral spirit that could go in any direction depending on how it was treated: Stored in oak to become whisky; filtered over and over again to become vodka; infused with juniper to become gin or caraway to become schnapps. Strathleven distils its spirit five times to achieve the highest possible alcoholic strength and then chill-filters at −15°C, at which temperature it becomes gelid and viscous. The purity thus achieved goes far beyond anything those early malt distillers could ever have dreamed of; but even so there is that

> [Strathleven's] aim, from first firing up their custom-made copper pot still on 13th April 2006, was to produce the purest possible spirits—not just whisky, but gin and vodka as well—entirely from Scottish malt.

look backward to the earliest distilling practices that Scotland's new-wave craft distillers always seem to have in mind.

...there is that look backward to the earliest distilling practices that Scotland's new-wave craft distillers always seem to have in mind.

None more so than Loch Ewe, where the first spirit flowed on 20th June that year. Founders Frances Oates and John Clotworthy were already whisky legends thanks to the 700+ single malts stocked at their hotel, the Drumchork Lodge at Aultbea; but then they conceived a burning passion for discovering more about whisky as their ancestors had distilled it in the bothie years of the 18th and early 19th centuries. Loch Ewe was therefore planned not just as a working distillery but as a laboratory too. Its first departure from established practice was to use a still of a mere 120 L (or 31 US gallons), which is about the right size for an illicit distillery of the 1700s. Next, they researched and resurrected a fermentation regime, still familiar to Bourbon distillers, which almost certainly travelled from the Highlands to Kentucky with Scottish exiles in the early 19th-century Clearances. (It's also the method used to make marc in France and grappa in Italy from grape pomace). This is simply to pitch the mash without troubling to strain it off the malt grist first, a very efficient method of giving the yeast access to all the extracted sugar rather than just some of it. This fast and furious fermentation yields a ferocious amount of heat (which must have been a welcome bonus in a bothie distillery in winter!), a wash of twice the normal strength, and low wines of 40% or more alcohol by volume. Finally, Loch Ewe does not mature its spirit; and as the law says it isn't whisky until it's rested in oak for at least three years, Loch Ewe's spirit is not sold as whisky. John Clotworthy maintains, and very credibly, that the illicit distillers of the 18th century didn't sit politely on their stocks of highly illegal spirit for three years but offloaded it as soon as they could, and that Loch Ewe is merely following their example. He might perhaps have tried doing what we know the smugglers are known to have done to make unaged spirit more potable, which was to rectify it with herbs and spices; but then he'd have been making gin.

After the initial rush of four distilleries in two years there was something of a hiatus when only two were founded in four years. Mark Tayburn's Abhainn Dearg, opened in 2008 on the island of Lewis in the Outer Hebrides, is a farm distillery very much along the lines of Daftmill and Kilchoman where as much as possible is done on site. Crossbill, though, fits no pattern and is entirely *sui generis*. Founded in a row of old chicken sheds up a farm track in a forest near Aviemore in 2010, it is the private world of former architect Jonathan Engels. The remote location was determined by the proximity of an ancient plantation of juniper, and Crossbill Gin is itself something of an oddity in that it uses only two botanicals: the juniper, and locally gathered rosehip.

This temporary check to craft distilling's progress is fairly easily explained by reference to the dates: It coincides with the global financial crisis that nearly destroyed the world's banking system, when both business confidence and the availability of credit were at a low ebb. Once the worst of it was over, though, Scottish craft distilling rebooted a little hesitantly and then went into overdrive, helped by a decade-long freeze in spirits duty (the Chancellor during those years being Gordon Brown… a Scot!) and even more by a shift of attitude on the part of customs, which had been prodded during the years of the financial crisis into conceding that revenue-raising businesses should be encouraged, not deterred.

Dunnet Bay, the first of the new crop, was founded in 2012 almost as a cottage industry by Martin and Claire Murray in Claire's home village of Dunnet on the Scottish mainland's north coast. Like Crossbill, their unique selling proposition was locally gathered botanicals including rose root and sea buckthorn. But given the economic circumstances, no bridges were burnt in the realization of their long-held ambition: Martin kept on working as a self-employed oil industry consultant, which left him enough downtime to tend the still while ensuring a steady income.

Call Martin Murray prudent or call him hesitant, but after him the Scottish craft brewing scene was dazzlingly illuminated by the glare of bridges being

> Abhainn Dearg, opened in 2008 on the island of Lewis in the Outer Hebrides, is a farm distillery...where as much as possible is done on site

gleefully burnt. Three more distilleries opened in 2013; an astonishing seven in 2014; five in 2015. And they came in all shapes and sizes. Two at least might classify as boutique distilleries:

Three more distilleries opened in 2013; an astonishing seven in 2014; five in 2015. And they came in all shapes and sizes.

Edinburgh Gin (2014) is actually in the bar of a high-end hotel, on display behind glass panels, while Summerhall (2013), also in Edinburgh, is part of an arts and retail complex carved out of an old veterinary hospital and although it doesn't actually have its own bar, it pipes its gin into the pub next door! Arbikie Estate and Ogilvy Spirits (both 2012) are both farm distilleries. Glasgow Distillery Company (2015) is a big concern headed by very experienced businessmen who are traditionally focused on creating top-class single malts both for bottling and for supplying to blender as fillings. A great many—Annadale, Ardnamurchan, Ballindalloch, Shetland (all 2014), and Isle of Harris and Kingsbarns (both 2015)—were conceived with the tourist very firmly in mind.

And then finally there are the nutters, GBS's unreasonable men, the entrepreneurs who run on enthusiasm, and who like Frances Oates and John Clotworthy of Loch Ewe and Jonathan Engel of Crossbill are prepared to take huge risks on the back of nothing more solid than passion. At Strathearn (2013), systems manager Tony Reeman-Clark and team-building specialist Stuart McMillan, both whisky fanatics, have created a base from which to spread the message, experimenting with different botanicals in their gins (in 2015 they brought out 12 entirely different small-batch gins) and different finishes for their whiskies and running three and five-day training courses for people as fanatical as themselves. Tony is also the founder of the Scottish Craft Distillers Association, which has already become very active and very effective in a life (at time of writing) of less than two years. Dark Matters (2015), not just Scotland's but Britain's only dedicated rum distillery, was established almost in a fit of pique by rum-loving brothers John and Jim McEwen after Jim couldn't find a distillery tour to go on while on vacation in the Dominican Republic. North Berwick (2013) owes its existence to disenchanted lawyer Steve Muir's experiments with botanicals using an adapted pressure-cooker in the kitchen as a makeshift rectifying still. And at Eden Mill (2015), Britain's only brewery-distillery (so far), Scott Ferguson is making whisky with different brewing malts including chocolate and crystal (he also makes hopped gin!).

As the brewing industry discovered 30 years ago, this sort of experiment and innovation is something you can only get away with in genuinely small-batch factories where one failure won't break the bank. With small-scale equipment you can also be far more flexible in your choice of operating spaces, which in turn offers the opportunity to tie production and retail together as fully integrated operations—in short, to create boutique distilleries, whether with visitor centers, cafes, and shops, or as fully fledged bars and restaurants where the public are always part of the show and are always likely to be surprised. And indeed all seven of the whisky distilleries that have been granted planning permission but have not yet opened at time of writing have tourism written into their business plans, and the SCDA sees a public interface as an essential part of the business.

"All the different trends point to more and more and smaller and smaller distilleries in the future," says Reeman-Clark. "We have people of all backgrounds, not all of them with huge sums to invest, being attracted to the industry; we have a regulatory authority that is becoming more and more co-operative; we have a sector that is very innovative and dynamic. We look forward to more distilleries opening as boutique bars in the future and we believe they will do very well.

"You only have to look at the craft brewing sector: People said that a growth-rate of two new breweries a week couldn't be sustained, and they were right: it's four a week!"

PART THREE
Whisky Tours

Abhainn Dearg

Ardnamurchan

Scotland's majestic scenery, rich and varied wildlife, and unique heritage may be its most-loved charms. But no Scottish trip would be complete without at least one distillery tour.

More than that: whisky distilleries have been built all over Scotland—on tiny islands, in wild and lonely glens, in picturesque town centers—so building your holiday around distillery visits is both a practical and a delightful way of discovering the country's many faces.

Two-thirds of Scotland's 100 or so malt whisky distilleries now welcome the public. The facilities on offer and operational arrangements in place, however, differ widely from distillery to distillery. Some have fully fledged visitor centers with cafés, gift shops, and tours of different durations and prices; a few even have accommodation! At the other end of the spectrum, many only offer basic tours by arrangement (with the plus that your tour guide is less likely to be a professional tour guide and more likely to be one of the distillery staff). Some are open year-round; others only during peak holiday times. So before planning your visit, always check the website, and preferably double-check by ringing ahead as well.

Anyone who is used to the historical and frankly arbitrary division of Scotland into whisky "regions" might be a little surprised that this guide pretty much dispenses with them. That is because it is intended as a practical tour guide: I have tried (although, thanks to geography and history, not always with success) to divide those distilleries that welcome visitors into clusters, each one centered on an interesting and attractive town or resort that offers accommodation, wining and dining, and other attractions as well—not necessarily related to whisky!

Any bars and hotels mentioned are included on the basis of common consent and widespread acclaim: It would be quite impossible for a single author to present the same sort of detailed, authoritative and up-to-date listings that the hundreds of volunteer contributors to the *Good Pub Guide* and the *Good Beer Guide* can, so apologies in advance for any disappointments.

The tours are arranged, for no very good reason, in a clockwise fashion starting at Gretna Green.

Southwest Scotland

Southwest Scotland was once studded with whisky distilleries, but there are only two now that welcome visitors—and one of those only opened in 2014. But they are the closest to England and therefore the easiest for Sassenachs to visit, and if you were on holiday in the Lake District you could almost visit them both in a single day-trip (provided you were prepared to get up really early).

But Dumfries & Galloway has so much to offer that it deserves a week or even two. As with so many parts of Scotland, the region's real attraction is the great outdoors. The **Galloway Forest Park** is 300 square miles of comparative wilderness with outdoor activities including (of course) hiking over the hills and through the woods; mountain biking at Glentrool and Kirroughtree; golf; deerstalking and salmon fishing (for the well-heeled); and wildlife to be spotted including ospreys on Wigtown Sands.

There's plenty of history and heritage, as well. **Wigtowns Parish Church**, for instance, has a Celtic cross dating from the 10th or 11th century; but far older than that is the ruined **Whithorn Priory**, 12 miles to the south. This is one of the great historical landmarks in Scotland's Christian history: It's where St. Ninian established his mission in the early 5th century and started the conversion of the Scots—who being on the wrong side of Hadrian's Wall had never been converted by the Romans.

Older still are the many Bronze Age stone circles and standing stones such as **Torhouse** that dot the surrounding hills, and there are medieval ruins to inspect too. The walled garden at the **Old Place of Mochrum**—a medieval tower house largely rebuilt in Victorian times—is well worth a visit if your fingers tend to green.

This is all very well and good, but it doesn't seem to offer much for the whisky tourist. Fear not, though: Dumfries is home to the awesome wine merchant and cigar shop **TB Watson** (11-17 English Street) which numbers 800 whiskies including many exclusive bottlings among its huge range of wines and spirits, holds regular tasting sessions, and also trades on the Internet as The Drambusters.

The **Cavens Arms** at 20 Buccleuch Street, the **New Bazaar** at 39 White Sands, and the **Tam o' Shanter** at 115 Queensberry Street also stock good ranges of single malts. The rest of the 75 miles of A714 and A75 that separate Bladnoch from Annandale are not, it has to be admitted, particularly promising hunting grounds for the whisky devotee, although the comfortingly solid **Galloway Arms Hotel** in Victoria Street, Newton Stewart, has a pretty impressive 120 malts in its lounge and another 30 in its public bar.

Annandale

■ *Annandale*

Annan DG12 5LL. 01461 207817
annandaledistillery.com

The nearest distillery to England is also, in a sense, one of Scotland's newest. Annandale is a mere seven miles up the A75 from Gretna: Turn right on to the B722 just north of the town of Annan, and about half a mile up on your left is a lane leading to a group of imposing stone buildings whose purpose is quickly revealed by a tall chimney and pagoda-style roof. But if this is such a new distillery, you ask, how come it's so obviously old?

Actually, Annandale was one of the rush of distilleries opened after the 1823 Excise Act: The original buildings date to 1830. Over the years it was extended and expanded—hence the pagoda maltings—but like so many others it was mothballed immediately after World War I. A few years later it became a farm and the maltings were used as a grain-dryer, a purpose for which they were ideally suited.

By 2006 the grand old buildings were disused and near-derelict. That's when international industrial research gurus David Thompson and Theresa Church stumbled across the place, and since they had always contemplated running a distillery that was also a visitor attraction, they bought it and spent over £10m on a long and painstaking restoration. The first spirit ran in November 2014 and at the same time a moderately Burns-themed (he was, after all, an excise officer in Dumfries for most of his adult life) cafe was opened.

No mature whisky is available yet, but Annandale bottles its new make spirit in peated and unpeated versions under the name Rascally Liquor.

Shop. Café. Four levels of tour. Ring ahead to book.

■ *Bladnoch*

Wigtown, DG8 9AB. 01988 402605
bladnoch.co.uk

Nestling on the banks of the little river of the same name and surrounded by low grassy hills, Bladnoch's air of serene tranquillity belies its checkered history. Founded by local brothers John and Thomas McClelland in 1817, it went along nicely in the 19th century but, like so many others, hit hard times in the early 20th and had been closed for six years when it was bought by Dumville's, a Northern Irish distillery company. From then on it was a stop-start affair, with the new owners investing heavily and being hit first by World War I and then by the Great Depression. It worked irregularly, rarely broke even, and closed in 1937.

In 1956, with the post-war economy recovering, it was reopened and reequipped, only to fall silent again in 1980. Then in 1983 Bell's bought it and started up again; but in 1987 Bell's was sold to United Distillers which included Bladnoch in the 1993 cull that did for Rosebank.

That would probably have been it for Scotland's most south-westerly distillery if the place hadn't been spotted by a Northern Irish senior civil servant, Raymond Armstrong, who was actually looking

Bladnoch river view

for a holiday home but fell in love with it, bought it, and in 2000 re-started production. Part of the plan was always to make Bladnoch as visitor-friendly as possible: Soon its tours, visitor center and legend-ary shop were attracting 30,000 tourists a year, and for a time it also ran a three-day hands-on Whisky School for the true enthusiast.

Sadly, Bladnoch's bad luck struck again in 2014 when the venture went into receivership; but in 2015 it was bought by Australian businessman David Pryor, and although the tours and the whisky school have been suspended (temporarily, we hope!) the shop and visitor center are open as usual.

Shop and Visitor Center, 10 am to 5 pm, Monday through Friday, year-round.

Glasgow

Glasgow has been striving to rehabilitate itself ever since it was immortalized as the poverty-stricken domain of razor gangs and street violence in the 1935 novel *No Mean City*. The industrial decline and dereliction of the 1960s to the 1980s didn't help, but in the last 30 years this most handsome of Victorian imperial cities has turned itself round almost completely.

Helped by its 1990 stint as European Capital of Culture, Glasgow has emerged as a world-class center for the arts: Scotland's national theatre, national ballet, and national orchestra are all based here, not in Edinburgh. Adjoining the theatre district, the bohemian chic of the **Merchant City** and the cornucopian shopping of the **West End** create a buzz of affluent pleasure-seeking more overtly hedonistic than the refined gentility of the capital.

Glasgow's whisky heritage is also very different from Edinburgh's. As a major international port looking out beyond the Clyde to the markets of the world—the Empire's Second City, as it was known—Glasgow became the headquarters of almost all the major blending and bottling concerns. And as an industrial city, it quickly progressed beyond the quirky idiosyncrasies of malt whisky distilling and by the end of the 1920s was turning out vast quantities of neutral grain spirit and nothing else from big super-efficient factories. Apart from the brief existence of the Kinlaich malt distillery within the huge Strathclyde grain distillery in the Gorbals—Kinlaich closed in 1975 to allow Strathclyde to expand—Glasgow produced no malt until July 2014, when the independent Glasgow Distillery Company fired up its gleaming copper stills (a first release is planned for 2018) to become the first in a new wave of craft distillers who are putting Glasgow back on the malt whisky map.

Until that moment Strathclyde had been the city's only distillery since its last competitor, Port Dundas, closed in 2010. Nevertheless, Glasgow has always had plenty to offer the whisky-loving visitor. **Robert Graham Ltd.** at 10-14 West Nile Street is the doyen of specialist whisky shops, having been around since 1874. As well as selling a huge range of malts it is also an independent bottler and, aptly enough, is perhaps Scotland's leading retailer of fine cigars. Buchanan Street has not one but two branches of **The Whisky Shop**, one in Buchanan Galleries and one in Princes Square; and a highly regarded newcomer is **Tam's Drams** at 1134 Argyle Street.

As for whisky bars, in the city center there's the magnificent **Pot Still** in Hope Street, a mercifully short stagger from the theatres; the **Bon Accord** with its 350 bottles on display in North Street; and (just to the southeast of the center itself) the cozy and relaxed **Scotia** in Stockwell Street. Most of the action is a little out west, though: **The Ubiquitous Chip** in Ashton Lane, Hillhead, is famous for its food and beer as well as its whiskies; **Dram!** at 232-246 Woodlands Rd. is close to the university and very lively as a result; and the **Ben Nevis** at 1147 Argyle Street is handily close to Tam's Drams and is renowned for its live Celtic music.

Auchentoshan Distillery; photo ©Peter Devlin

■ *Auchentoshan*
Dalmuir, Clydebank G81 4SJ. 01389 878561
auchentoshan.com

Thought to have been founded in about 1800, Auchentoshan is not only the oldest-attested malt distillery in this part of the world but was, for a while, the last survivor.

Just 10 miles from Glasgow city center, Auchentoshan was once in open countryside, enjoying pleasant views over the Clyde. Modernity has rather caught up with Dalmuir, though: It may be right on the edge of the Glasgow conurbation, but with the A82 roaring by, the massive Erskine Bridge only yards away, the approach run into Glasgow airport directly overhead, and the whole area blanketed with housing and industrial estates it's hardly what you'd call bucolic.

Nevertheless the distillery buildings themselves, erected in 1875, are very much of their type and not at all unattractive, and Auchentoshan is extremely visitor-friendly with conference facilities, a well-stocked gift shop, and a variety of tours going right up to the Ultimate Auchentoshan Experience that includes comparative tastings and a sensory awareness masterclass.

It's a tiny bit hard to get to, despite its urban setting: From Glasgow take the A82 northbound and Auchentoshan has its own sliproad; coming towards Glasgow on the A82, take the first left after the Erskine Bridge and double back on yourself. The trick is to slow down and concentrate as you approach Dalmuir from either direction so that you don't miss the turn.

Shop. Conference facilities. Four standard tours a day; also personal tours and premium tours. Ring ahead to book.

■ *Deanston*
Doune FK16 6AG. 01786 843010
deanstonmalt.com

Strictly speaking a Highland distillery, Deanston is so handy for Glasgow (A80, M80, A84) that it can safely be included on the Lowland itinerary. And although it's a 30-mile trip it's one that's well worth making, especially if your interests embrace industrial archaeology and heritage as well as whisky!

The distillery buildings were originally a cotton mill built by the father of the Industrial Revolution himself, Richard Arkwright, in 1785 and powered by the waters of the busy little River Teith on whose banks it stands. Steam-powered woollen sheds were added in 1836, but in the 1940s the whole mill reverted to water power with the installation of hydro-electric turbines—again, driven by the River Teith. Only in 1965, as Britain's textile industry declined,

Deanston on the River Teith

Deanston casks

did the mill's owner—global tea and cotton concern James Finlay & Co.—decide to convert it into a distillery in a joint venture with Glasgow whisky broker Brodie Hepburn (which had earlier built Tullibardine). The work included turning the magnificent vaulted woollen sheds into huge and unique maturation warehouses.

The venture was sold to Invergordon in 1972, but Deanston was closed 10 years later and remained silent until it was bought and reopened by the Glasgow-based distiller Burn Stewart, owner of

Bunnahabhainn and Tobermory. The three distilleries are now part of the South African-owned Distell conglomerate.

Despite its heritage Deanston—still powered by its hydroelectric turbines—was closed to the public until 2012, when a £600,000 visitor center was opened. So today you can see those cathedral-like warehouses and their rows of oak casks for yourself—and you should!

Visitor center. Cafe. Five grades of tour up to Distillery Manager's Tour. Phone ahead to book/ensure availability.

Glasgow Distillery

■ Glasgow Distillery
243 Great George Street, Glasgow G2 4QY
0141 404 7191. glasgowdistillery.com

When business partners Liam Hughes, Mike Hayward, and Ian McDougall decided to open a new malt whisky distillery in Glasgow, they thought it fitting to revive the name of the company that operated the last one—Dundashill, which closed in 1902.

Dundashill was founded in 1770 beside the Forth & Clyde canal—on the same basin, in fact, as the Port Dundas Distillery which went on to become the biggest in Scotland. It operated for much of its life under the Glasgow Distillery Company banner, and was one of the 60 small independents that went bust as a result of the collapse of Pattison Brothers, a huge blender and bottler that failed suddenly and unexpectedly, owing its suppliers thousands. In 1903 the site was bought by the Distillers Company, and although most of the buildings were either demolished or converted into flats and offices, part of Dundashill worked on as a cooperage until 2009.

The connection between the two Glasgow Distillery Companies is more symbolic than anything else—the new GDC's actual production site is two miles away from Dundashill, at the Hillington Business Park on the borders of Glasgow and Renfrew—but one thing the two distilleries do share is a water source, Loch Katrine, far away in the Trossachs. Since the mid-19th century Katrine water has been channeled to Glasgow via two 35-mile aqueducts: At the time the new supply eradicated cholera and typhoid from the burgeoning city, and now, 150 years on, its quality is still rated as second to none for distilling purposes.

The distillery's one-tonne mash tun, four 5,000-L fermenters, and two stills (Tara and Mhairi) were designed, commissioned, and installed under the watchful eye of David Robertson, formerly Master Distiller at Macallan. The new make won a Spirit of the Future award, and the first cask was filled in March 2015, with a limited release scheduled for late 2018.

GDC is very much a working distillery, modern, functional, and intended to supply fillings to blenders as well as its own bottlings; but if your trip is only taking you to Glasgow and you want to see how Scotch whisky is made, they'll be only too glad to lay on a private tour just for you!

Private tours strictly by appointment. Contact Heather Findlay at heather.findlay@glasgowdistillery.com for details

■ Glengoyne

Dumgoyne, Killearn G63 9LB. 01360 550254
glengoyne.com

Is Glengoyne a Lowland or a Highland distillery? It's a moot point, and one to argue about over a friendly dram. For the distillery actually straddles the imaginary Greenock-Dundee dividing line, and while the whisky here is distilled in the Highland region, it's aged in the Lowland.

Glengoyne

And the best place to have this friendly argument is Glengoyne itself. Only 14 miles from Glasgow on the A81 Aberfeldy road, its setting makes an interesting backdrop to the debate. For the dividing line here is as much geographical as imaginary, with the Earl's Seat on the Campsie Fells rising to over 1,900 feet and a 50-foot waterfall crashing down the sheer basalt slopes of Dumgoyne providing the distillery's mashing liquor. It helps that Glengoyne is frequently rated as one of the prettiest distilleries in Scotland.

Given its setting and its proximity to Glasgow, it's no surprise that the 180-year-old distillery—founded by a local landowning family to displace the "small stills" that flourished in the hills hereabouts—is one of the most visited in Scotland. It's only half-an-hour's drive from Glasgow, but if you have no car the No. 10 bus from Buchanan Street bus station stops right at the distillery gate. Tales of a helipad on the site are exaggerated, though—there's a field nearby where helicopters sometimes land, but it's nothing to do with Glengoyne!

Visitor center. Shop. Seven levels of tour from standard to Century of Whisky. Open seven day—tours on the hour 10 am to 3 pm, March through November; 10 am to 4 pm, December through February. Ring ahead for availability, group tours, and premium tours.

■ *Strathleven*

Vale of Leven Ind Est, Dumbarton G82 3PD. 01389 298755
enquiries@strathlevendistillers.com

Founded in 2006, Strathleven was one of the earliest of the new wave of craft distillers in Scotland and was inspired by curiosity about the very earliest distilled drinks in northern Europe.

Whisky, gin, and vodka all originated with the discovery in the 15th or possibly even the 14th century that it was possible to distil a spirit from malt liquor that was every bit as good as a distillate of wine—and in northerly climes it was much, much cheaper. The members of this family of malt-based spirits gradually diverged with the discovery first that potatoes yielded a passable distillate, and second that the column still made miscellaneous unmalted grains a viable source of spirits, too.

Then in 2006 Ricky Christie, former managing director of the pioneering Speyside craft distillery (and son of the founder), decided to reunite the spirit family and with business partner Oliver Storrie founded Strathleven to do just that. From a near identical malt liquor-based ethanol they first created Valt Vodka (vodka/malt—geddit?), distilled not three times but five and chilled to –15°C (5° F) before filtration; then, in 2013, Gilt gin (same joke), and now (late 2016) a 10-year-old single malt to be called either simply Strathleven or "Faith" because, says Oliver, you need plenty of it to lay down a whisky for 10 years!

The distillery is on an industrial estate and has no facilities for tourists. But the partners welcome groups of visitors by prior appointment, especially fairly knowledgeable visitors who share their obsession.

Tours strictly by prior arrangement.

Campbeltown including *Arran*

To visit Campbeltown, towards the southern end of the Kintyre peninsula on the west coast of Scotland, is to get a rare reminder of what small towns were like 50 years ago. Not because it's in any way backward, but because it's so remote.

Towns of Campbeltown's size—it has about 5,000 inhabitants—in more populous regions have long ago lost all facilities beyond a handful of pubs, a convenience store or small supermarket and one or two other shops, a village hall, and a takeaway or two. Campbeltown, though, is nearly 40 miles by winding road from Tarbert at the northern neck of the peninsula, so there's no giant supermarket or retail park to monopolize the local custom. As a result, the town still has plenty of independent shops, pubs, and even a cinema of its own (the rather startlingly Art Deco **Wee Picture House**, Scotland's oldest and celebrating its centenary in 2013) just as every country town did 60 years ago. Campbeltown also hosts the **Mull of Kintyre Music Festival** every August. Founded in 1993 and held in various venues round the town, it features mainly Scottish and Northern Irish traditional music but performers have included Deacon Blue and the Stranglers.

Campbeltown was planted (and modestly named) in 1667 by the local landowner, Archibald Campbell, Earl of Argyll, on the site of a fishing village called Kinlochkilkerran—the cell of St. Kieran at the head of the loch—to exploit the excellent natural harbour on which it stood. It was a shrewd move. The fishing fleet grew; a shipbuilding industry sprang up; and coal mined at Machrihanish a few miles across the peninsula was shipped to the harbor at first by canal, then by a light railway that closed only in 1932.

But there's more to Cambeltown than its industrial heritage. There's the climate, for a start: The Gulf Stream warms the whole coast, so you'll see palm trees lining the streets; and in the late 19th century it even became something of a fashionable resort. Many handsome pieds-a-terre were built by prosperous Glaswegians who arrived for their holidays by ferry, and the fine Victorian municipal buildings include the town hall with its white spire and the old library, now the museum.

Set as it is between beautiful countryside and the sea, Campbeltown is a center both for stunning walks along the **Kintyre Way** and for watching seabirds, seals, and dolphins either from the **Machrihanish Bird Observatory** or from the fast boat services based in the harbor. The island of **Davaar** (accessible by causeway at low tide) is definitely of interest: In 1887 one of its seven sea-caves suddenly sprouted a painting of the crucifixion, which some local people took to be miraculous until it turned out to have been the work of a local artist, Archie McKinnon. McKinnon claimed to have been inspired by a holy vision; but people who thought they'd been duped weren't impressed, and he was chased out of town.

Campbeltown's deep natural harbor made it a magnet for whisky distillers. Coal and barley arrived by sea; whisky left by sea. By the late 19th century Campbeltown whiskies were exported direct to markets all over the world.

Over the years Campbeltown has seen 34 distilleries come and go, and at its height in the 1880s, 25 of them were operating at once—enough to classify the town as a whisky region in its own right. World wars, the Depression, and Prohibition wore them down until eventually only Springbank was left. For a while the Scotch Whisky Association declassified Campbeltown as a region; now there's a resurgence in the town, with three distilleries producing five malts, and it's been reinstated. None of the three has a visitor center, but the town's **Heritage Centre** gives plenty of insight into distilling's history and renaissance here.

Naturally the town is packed with pubs, bars, and restaurants stocking a wider range of whiskies than their English opposite numbers would: the **Feathers Inn** in Cross Street claims a whisky list of 140; the **Black Sheep Bar** in the very handsome **Royal Hotel** on the harbor also has a good selection. But with at least 700 bottles,

> Over the years Campbeltown has seen 34 distilleries come and go, and at its height in the 1880s, 25 of them were operating at once — enough to classify the town as a whisky region in its own right.

the **Ardshiel Hotel** in Kilkerran Road takes the biscuit. Its bar-back is a veritable crystal palace of glittering whisky-bottles, so densely packed there's no room to display the hotel's many trophies and awards. And of course, as the capital city of the Mitchell whisky empire there's a branch of **Cadenhead's** with a tasting room in Union Street.

The Isle of Arran and its single distillery are often lumped in with Campbeltown, not because there's any historical or geographical connection, but because there's a ferry in summer from Claonaig just up the coast to the island's capital, Lochranza.

Arran is not a large island, but has an important place in the history of the study of evolution. People may think that it was Charles Darwin who first seriously challenged the Biblical view of history and prehistory, but it wasn't. It was the pioneering Scottish geologist James Hutton, who after studying rock formations on Arran, concluded that the Earth was not a few thousand years old as computed from the Old Testament, but a few billion. And this was in the 1780s, nearly 30 years before Darwin was even born. **Hutton's Unconformity**, the rock formation on which he based his theorizing, is still shown to visitors as the place where—you could argue—the modern world-picture came into being.

Arran (not to be confused with Aran off the west coast of Ireland, where the bulletproof sweaters come from) is still known as the geologist's paradise, and has a field studies center where generations of schoolchildren have come to look dutifully at pieces of stone. Its center is slashed diagonally by the Highland Boundary Fault, which divides the island into a rugged, almost mountainous, northwest (four corbetts, of which the highest is Goat Fell at 2,866 feet) and a rather less rugged but still pretty up-and-down southeast. It is—as are so many of the places where whisky is made—a paradise not only for geologists but for anyone who loves the majestic outdoors.

The wildlife that mountain bikers and walkers—either on the coastal trail or on the hillier interior paths—are likely to encounter includes not only the ubiquitous red deer but also grey seals, sea otters, and golden eagles; and for the den-

> [Arran is] a paradise not only for geologists but for anyone who loves the majestic outdoors.

drologist Arran also has three subspecies of whitebeam that grow nowhere else.

Most of these pleasures will be enjoyed pretty much in solitude, since Arran is a lot less populous than it used to be. It has been settled—and quite thickly, judging by the cairns, stone circles, barrows and forts—since the Neolithic, and its fortress-like location at the mouth of the Firth of Clyde made it a place of strategic importance. St. Brendan, the Irish monk who is reputed to have reached America in his leather boat, founded a monastery here in the 6th century, from which to convert the mainland; the Viking rulers of Man seized Arran five centuries later and held it until 1266, when the Scottish monarchy managed to regain control. Robert Bruce, during his vicissitudes of the 1320s, chose it as a place first to retreat to and then to rally at: The cave where he was, according to legend, given fresh heart by observing the pertinacity of the spider, is at Blackwaterfoot on the west coast.

The clearances took quite a toll on Arran, though. The Duke of Hamilton packed most of his crofting tenants off to Canada, where he promised that ample farmland was awaiting them. (It wasn't.) The population fell from 6,600 in 1831 to 4,700 in 1851 (It carried on falling until 1991, since when it has started growing again, and now stands at just above 5,000). Sheep and deer replaced the little fields of oats and barley—and with the crofters went the distilleries… until now. And to see how the Duke lived while he was evicting the crofters, visit his home, **Brodick Castle**, with its country park and gardens.

Lochranza is tiny and has little in the way of tourist facilities, but the bar at the **Lochranza Hotel** stocks a respectable range of malts. Nobody seems to know how many, but it's well over 100.

Glengyle

■ *Glengyle*
Glengyle Street, PA28 6EX. 01586 551710
kilkerran.com

Much of the history of Campbeltown distilling is bound up with the fortunes and fallings-out of the Mitchell family, which founded Springbank in the 1820s. Glengyle was established in 1872 by William Mitchell, brother of the John who was running Springbank at the time, as a result of some now-obscure quarrel.

The distillery was sold out of family hands in 1919, only to confound its new owners' hopes and close in 1925. Its fate thereafter included use as a rifle range, and attempts to reopen it in the 1940s and 1950s came to nothing.

Then in 2000 the building was bought by Hedley Wright, current scion of the Mitchell dynasty and proprietor of Springbank, who re-equipped it using as much salvaged equipment as possible. The two stills come from the Ben Wyvis malt distillery that operated from 1965 to 1977 within the huge Invergordon grain distilling complex on the east coast of Scotland.

The reborn Glengyle started operations in 2004, producing a malt under the name Kilkerran, as the Glengyle name belongs to someone else.

Tours only as part of Springbank tour or by appointment.

■ Glen Scotia
High Street, PA28 6DS.
01586 552288
glenscotia.com

Glen Scotia

Glen Scotia's fortunes mirror those of the town as a whole. The business was established in 1832 by a coppersmith, Robert Armour, who it seems had previously been perfectly happy to sell his four-part stills (vessel, head, arm, and worm) to farmers just down from the hills, no questions asked, but decided to turn distiller himself once it was legitimized. As improvements in technology and transport created a big demand for whisky, Glen Scotia prospered and in the 1890s was rebuilt and extended.

Prohibition in the US from 1919 cut off a key market, while Britain's return to the gold standard in 1925 made exports more expensive generally. In 1928 Glen Scotia became one of the 20 Campbeltown distilleries that closed between the wars and is supposedly haunted by the ghost of its then owner, the 81-year-old Duncan MacCallum, who was found drowned two years later having been tricked out of £40,000 by a gang of fraudsters. Unlike other Campbeltown distilleries, though, Glen Scotia reopened in 1933, the year Prohibition was repealed, supplying the very heavy, oily, peaty malt so prized by American blenders because it only needed to be sparingly used.

Since the war the distillery has changed ownership often in the perpetual corporate merry-go-round; in 1984 it was mothballed only shortly after a £1 million refurbishment. In the 1980s and 1990s it worked only sporadically but since 1999 has been open continuously, albeit producing nothing like its potential capacity.

Tours used to be strictly by arrangement, but in keeping with the times the whole place has been thoroughly spruced up, its gloomy grey and rather barrack-like street frontage has been livened up with a coat of whitewash, and the public are now welcome.

Shop and tasting room. Tours daily 11:30 am and 3pm. Book ahead.

Springbank kilning

■ *Springbank*

Well Close, PA28 6ET. 01586 551710
springbankwhisky.com

For many whisky-lovers, Springbank would be their last dram before dying. Of all Campbeltown's malt distilleries it has suffered fewest periods in mothballs—it was silent during the latter years of Prohibition and again, briefly, in the 1980s—and the reputation of today's whiskies is towering.

The distillery was founded by the Mitchell family in the 1820s and is still owned by a direct descendant. The family history, if televised, would rival the show "Dallas" as a melodramatic saga, with various brothers, sisters, aunts, uncles, cousins and in-laws owning at different stages Rieclachan, Glengyle, Drumore, Toberanrigh, and Longrow as well as Springbank itself and the merchant bottler William Cadenhead.

Family ownership and its high reputation allow Springbank the freedom to operate without compromise. It still has its own floor malting; its wash-still (the first still in the process) is direct-fired; it double- and triple-distills; it doesn't chill-filter in the bottling; it even refuses to colour-equalise different batches with a shot of caramel.

But Springbank doesn't only produce Springback. Occasionally it really peats its malt to make Longrow, part of whose old premises it has expanded into; and by way of contrast it has also revived the name of another long-gone Campbeltown distillery, Hazelburn, for an unpeated, triple-distilled malt of contrasting delicacy.

Shop. Standard tours twice daily Monday through Saturday, once on Sunday. Some tours include Glengyle. Also walking tours of Campbeltown. Ring ahead to book (the phone number is that of the distillery shop, so don't be thrown!).

Isle of Arran

■ *Isle of Arran*
Shore Rd, Lochranza KA27 8HJ. 01770 830264
arranwhisky.com

Before the clearances, Arran was home to a reputed 50 moonshiners whose products were much appreciated by mainland gentry, amongst whom they were referred to as "Arran waters." There were also a handful of legal distillers in the southern part of the island; but with their customers packed off to Canada they had all closed by 1837.

Nearly 150 years later Arran—and more specifically a little glen outside Lochranza on Arran's northern tip—was chosen by retired whisky industry executive Harold Currie as the stage for his return (evidently he had retired too early) partly because he had family ties to the island, partly because industry experts assured him that the water here was the best that could be had. The site was acquired in 1993 and the construction was funded partly by Mr. Currie and partly by the issue of 2,000 £450 bonds. Work was held up while a pair of golden eagles found a suitable nest nearby; but it paid off when the eagles staged an impromptu flypast at the official opening in July 1995.

Two years later the Queen herself cut the ribbon on the visitor center, to which a shop and restaurant have since been added. The distillery was always intended to be visitor-friendly, and as it is a compact and well-laid out operation the range of three tours— oak, copper, and gold—are genuinely educational as well as a great pleasure.

Shop. Restaurant. Visitor center. Seven daily tours (standard and copper); two gold tours. Ring ahead to book.

Islay & Jura

Depending on your point of view, Islay—the southernmost of the Inner Hebrides—is either impossibly remote or the center of your empire. Eighty miles by road plus a two-hour ferry journey from Glasgow, it can be a daunting trip for the modern holidaymaker. For a medieval warlord descended from Vikings, on the other hand, it was ideally positioned between western Scotland, the Hebrides, and Ireland, and was therefore a base from which his fleet could control a huge territory.

Islay is a great destination for lovers of the outdoors. Thanks to the gulf stream the climate is mild (don't be surprised when you spot the palm trees!), and there are great walks for all levels of fitness from flat coastal rambles that reveal little sandy coves and beaches to quite demanding upland hikes, the highest point being Beinn Bheigeir at a respectable 1,600 ft. At Machrie near the little airport there is (of course) golf; and there is bird watching: Not just the seabirds and wildfowl you'd expect, but mainland rarities such as choughs and corncrakes whose habitat has been preserved by low-intensity farming. There's a large **Royal Society for the Protection of Birds (RSPB) Reserve** on The Oa in the south of the island.

And there's history, lots of it. Standing as it does at a maritime crossroads, Islay has been inhabited since the end of the last ice age. The oldest human settlement dates from 7,500 BCE, and there are prehistoric remains from the middle stone age onwards, including **Cultoon Stone Circle.** Evidence of early Christianity is literally thick on the ground: St. Columba knew the place, according to a biography written in about 720 CE, and among the many Celtic Christian gravestones and crosses to be seen is **Kildalton High Cross**, dating to about 880 CE and the best-preserved of its kind in the whole of Scotland.

...Islay comprises 130 miles of coast punctuated by convenient harbors and surrounding 500 square miles of rugged hills and peat bog.

Jura, which is linked to Islay by a ferry that takes a mere five minutes to cross from Port Askaig to Feolin, is one of the great wildernesses of Scotland.

The historic centerpiece is the island settlement on **Loch Finlaggan**. More of a palace complex than a castle, it was the administrative capital of the MacDonalds, Lords of the Isles from the 14th to the 16th centuries, and more powerful at their height than the Kings of Scotland. The impressive ruins include a great hall or council chamber in which successive Lords were formally invested by whole parties of subservient bishops. The Lords' naval base was at **Dunnyvaig castle**, whose ruins can still be seen overlooking Lagavulin Bay on the south coast.

Memories of humbler life are preserved at the museum in the former **Free Church at Port Charlotte**, whose exhibits include a rare survival—a moonshine still from the era before whisky distilling was legalized. Whisky, of course, is also central to the main event in Islay's cultural calendar, the **Festival of Malt & Music** held in the last week of May. Events embracing arts and crafts, local cuisine (the seafood is epic), traditional music, and poetry are staged at many venues round the island, and most of the eight distilleries open their doors to the public.

To oversimplify, Islay comprises 130 miles of coast punctuated by convenient harbors and surrounding 500 square miles of rugged hills and peat bog. This made it the ideal spot for distillers when the modern whisky industry was created in the early 19th century: The barley arrived by sea; it was malted over local peat; it was mashed with pure mountain water; and the final product was shipped out across the world. The composition of the peat here is important: Islay's lack of woody material has produced a peat high in phenol and guaiacol, which gives its malts—especially Laphroaig—their smoky, almost medicinal character.

Jura, which is linked to Islay by a ferry that takes a mere five minutes to cross from Port Askaig to Feolin, is one of the great wildernesses of Scotland. It's about the same size as its southern neighbor but has a resident population of no more than 200 who are comfortably outnumbered by some 5,000 red deer. It's not only emptier than Islay, it's more rugged too: Beinn an Oir, the highest of the Paps of Jura (of which there are, curiously, three) rises to over 2,500 feet. The western coast is uninhabited and uninhabitable. The northern end is mostly moorland. Only the southeastern littoral, between the Paps and the sea, is much populated; and it's here that you'll find the one settlement, **Craighouse**, with the one hotel, the one shop, and the one distillery.

Jura is paradise for walkers, especially of the hardier sort for whom the ascent of the **Paps** is rewarded by astonishing views of Colonsay, Islay, Kintyre, even County Antrim on a good day, and all the scattered dozens of islets and rocks that lie between. The more privileged visitor might even be granted access to the deer-stalking and salmon-fishing owned by the lairds of the island's great estates. For the humbler sort there's the chance to spot all manner of wild-life—otters, wild goats, seals, and eagles, as well as deer—that is rare to the point of invisibility elsewhere in Britain.

It was not always thus. From the Mesolithic to the 16th century of our own era the island was well-peopled, and there are plentiful remains—duns, crannogs, hill forts, standing stones, cairns, crofts—to remind the modern visitor that this was once a thriving center of population and agriculture. Then came a civil war that followed the fall of the Macdonald Lords of the Isles as Campbells and Macleans strove to take over. Many Macdonald sympathizers were deported to the mainland. That was followed by the climate's 17th-century dip—the era of the Thames "frost fairs"—when many more island-ers emigrated to the American Colonies. Finally, in the 19th cen-tury, the Campbell lairds decided that sheep were more profitable than crofters and squeezed out most of the remaining population by means of outrageous rent rises. The crofters went to Canada, and Jura achieved its modern state of emptiness.

Most of what Jura has to offer the visitor is, therefore, outdoors. After the ascent of the Paps, the most popular walk is the long hike along the eastern coast past **Barnhill**, the isolated cottage where George Orwell spent his last TB-racked years cycling, sailing, and writing 1984, and on to the spectacular

> ...duns, crannogs, hill forts, standing stones, cairns, crofts—a reminder that this was once a thriving center of population and agriculture.

Corryvreckan whirlpool, which makes the strait separating the northern tip of Jura from the mainland all but impassable. But there are many less demanding activities including boat trips, days on palm-fringed sandy beaches (don't forget the Gulfstream!) and, of course, the distillery tour.

For the truly hardy, the 16-mile **Jura Fell Race** over seven summits including all three Paps is held every year in May. The record to beat is three hours and seven minutes. For the more laid-back, the island hosts a music festival every September.

It hardly needs saying that Islay, with its whisky-based economy, abounds with superbly stocked whisky bars, some of them absurdly so: **The Bowmore Hotel** in Jamieson Street, Bowmore, claims to have a range of 700+, while the **Lochside Whisky Lounge** on the haborfront nearby claims 300. Bowmore also has **Islay Whisky Shop** in Shore Street for a spot of take-home shopping. In Port Charlotte across the loch you'll find the **Lochindaal Hotel**, which has been in the same family for more than a century and has been building up an astonishing and surely invaluable collection of whiskies for most of that time. Port Charlotte is also home to the **Port Charlotte Hotel** which as well as stocking a noble selection of whiskies also organizes "Malt, Music, and Culture" tours of the island for its guests, taking in most of the distilleries. Elsewhere on Islay you'll find the **Port Bar** at the Port Askaig Hotel in Port Askaig, the **Islay Hotel** and the **White Hart** in Port Ellen... actually, you can scarcely move on Islay without tripping over a damned fine whisky bar, and to attempt to list them all would be a vain endeavor. On Jura, by contrast, there's just the one, the **Jura Hotel** right next door to the distillery, its palm-fringed lawn running down to the sea, which actually possesses more bottlings of Isle of Jura than the distillery does itself and has one special expression of its own that you can get nowhere else. Wherever you choose to eat and drink on Islay, though, you will discover one immutable truth: The seafood here is the best in the world.

Ardbeg

■ *Ardbeg*
Port Ellen, PA42 7EA. Tel 01496 302244
ardbeg.com

The last three miles of the A486 might well be called Whisky Boulevard, since this short stretch of road passes three of Islay's best-known distilleries: First Laphroaig; then Lagavulin; and finally, just where it turns into the narrow lane to Kindalton, Ardbeg.

Like many distilleries, Ardbeg was licensed in the early 19th century when legislative reform was driving the small semi-legal or plain illegal distiller out of business and favoring the formation of larger commercial concerns. The farmer here, John MacDougall, may have been a moonshiner himself—certainly the cove on which Ardbeg stands had previously been used by smugglers.

Ardbeg, although it was sold to a Glasgow bottling firm in 1838, was managed by members of the MacDougall family from its foundation in 1815 until it was sold to the US firm Hiram Walker in 1977. From then on, it went into a rapid decline. In 1980 its traditional floor-maltings was closed; in 1981 the distillery itself followed. It was reopened for small-scale production in 1989, only to close again a couple of years later.

Then in 1997 it was bought by the Highland distiller Glenmorangie and is now back in full production, turning out some of Islay's most gloriously and unapologetically peaty malt whiskies from a site in a rugged cove that seems to epitomize all the island's distilleries. The long, low warehouse fronting the sea—almost in the sea at high tide—is kept painted gleaming white as much to protect the old stone against the constant salt spray as for any aesthetic reason. At the end of its track and with scarcely a human habitation in sight it seems far remoter and more self-contained than it really is, and could be a Newfoundland or South Georgia whaling station just as easily as a Scottish distillery.

Shop. Restaurant. Tours with tastings every weekday morning an shorter tours every weekday afternoon. Ring to book.

Bowmore malting

■ *Bowmore*
School Street, Bowmore, PA43 7JS. 01496 810671
bowmore.com

Situated pretty much in the center of Islay's largest town, Bowmore claims the double distinction of being the oldest (legal) distillery on the island and also, for much of its history, the most go-ahead.

First mentioned in the records in 1779, Bowmore was founded by a local farmer named Simson who also described himself as a "merchant." The implication is that the above-board, taxpaying concern was intended to supply a much wider market than the mainly local trade of the illicit moonshiners. It must have done well, for in 1837 it was bought by a forward-looking farming family of German descent, the Mutters, who pulled it down and erected the existing rather military-looking buildings, which were perhaps the first on the island to use concrete in the construction. The Mutters also used their own iron-built steamship as transport.

Bowmore was closed during World War II, when it was a base for RAF Coastal Command flying boats, but reopened in 1950 and was later bought by a forward-looking independent entrepreneur, Stanley P. Morrison. As a gift to the town, he turned one of the warehouses into a swimming-pool warmed by waste heat from the stills.

This is one of the few Scottish distilleries where you can still see a traditional floor-maltings being worked. Its products are fruitier and less peaty than some Islay malts, and Bowmore was among the first to experiment in ageing whisky in old sherry casks.

Visitor center open year-round. Up to four tours a day Monday through Saturday, depending on season, without booking. Ring to book Craftman's Tours. Bowmore also has six holiday cottages in former distillery buildings.

■ *Bruichladdich*
Bruichladdich, PA49 7UN. 01496 850190
bruichladdich.com

Facing Bowmore across Loch Indaal, Bruichladdich—and spell it carefully, or you'll never find the website—had an unspectacular career starting in 1881 when it was built by Harvey's, a firm of Glasgow distillers, to supply bulk quantities of lightly peated malt whisky for blending.

Like many Scottish distilleries, it suffered from the loss of exports during Prohibition in America, and actually closed from 1929 to 1936. But other than that it just plodded on—its single malt was not even bottled until after World War II.

Corporate shenanigans of the 1960s through the 1990s saw it change hands several times until eventually its then parent company, Invergordon Distillers, was bought by Whyte & Mackay and the distillery was closed.

...much of the equipment and vattage [at Bruichladdich] the visitor will see is pretty much antique, extremely rare, and utterly fascinating.

In 2000, however, it was bought and reopened by an adventurous private consortium and began a new life as a kind of boutique distillery, avoiding the mass market but producing a number of individualistic and experimental short-run bottlings including—in a complete reversal of tradition—the world's peatiest malt, Octomore. It also now has a gin, The Botanist, whose botanicals are entirely locally sourced. The consortium sold it 12 years later to Cognac producer Remy Cointreau.

A happy side-effect of its several changes of ownership has been a lack of inward investment, so much of the equipment and vattage the visitor will see is pretty much antique, extremely rare, and utterly fascinating. It was all taken out and restored, piece by piece, after the distillery changed hands in 2000, and it's still operated by hand and eye: The only computers here are in the accounts office! The distillery also has its own cooperage, another rarity—and even more unusual, it's a new one which has only operated since 2004.

Shop. Six tours a day Monday through Friday, three on Saturday, two on Sunday, during summer season. Two tutored tastings a day. Ring to book.

■ *Bunnahabhain*
Bunnahabhainn, PA46 7RP. 01496 840646
bunnahabhain.com

Another one for careful spelling (note the tiny difference between the name of the distillery and the name of its village, "Bunnahabhainn"), Bunnahabhain has an almost identical provenance to Bruichladdich in that it was built in 1881 to supply large volumes (hence the size of some of the vessels) of lightly peated malt whisky to blenders; and, other than one or two periods in mothballs when demand was low, it has had a fairly uneventful career doing just that ever since.

The distillery's glory is its setting. The most northerly on the island, it sits a few miles up a single-track lane from Port Askaig amid a tiny hamlet of former workers' cottages, some of which are now run by the distillery's owners as holiday lets. The place is so remote—and Port Askaig, the nearest source of diversion, is no metropolis—that a holiday spent there would be a meditative experience indeed. Like all Islay's distilleries, Bunnahabhain sits on the sea

Bunnahabhain

front; unlike them, it still has its pier, built in 1887, at which steamers unloaded the necessary malt and loaded up with finished whisky.

Although famous for its unpeated malt, Bunnahabhain has recently introduced a much more peaty bottling, Toiteach—which is Gaelic for "smoky."

Shop. Three standard tours a day, Monday through Friday, March through October. Also VIP tours. All tours must be booked in advance.

■ *Caol Ila*
Port Askaig, PA46 7RL. 01496 302760
discovering-distilleries.com

Like its nearest neighbor, Bunnahabhain, Caol Ila enjoys a spectacular if somewhat hard of access setting at the end of a steep and winding track on the sea shore facing Jura. It is somewhat older than Bunnahabain, though, having been founded in 1846, 23 years after the legislation that all but hounded the illicit moonshiners out of existence while making large-scale distilling a commercial possibility.

Caol Ila used to be one of the most architecturally distinguished of Islay distilleries, having been complete rebuilt in the grand Gothic style in 1879, when phylloxera was devastating the French brandy industry and malt whisky was overtaking Cognac in popularity.

The Victorian distillery, alas, was almost completely demolished in 1972, save for one warehouse, to make way for a massively expanded new one. Caol Ila, being a full-bodied and, according to some, even oily malt, was much in demand for blending since a little goes a long way, and at that time whisky production was rapidly expanding. Little of its output was bottled as a single malt; but since those days

Caol Ila

matters have been put right and in the last decade various expressions of Caol Ila have won international gold medals, prompting proprietor Diageo to include it in its Classic Malts range.

Visitor center. Shop. Standard tours twice a day Tuesday through Saturday in winter, five times a day, seven days, in summer. Premium tours also available. Phone to book.

■ Kilchoman

Rockside Farm, Bruichladdich, PA49 7UT
01496 850011. kilchomandistillery.com

If Kilchoman looks like a fairly typical modern arable farm, that's because it *is* a fairly typical modern arable farm. For Islay's most westerly and smallest distillery was founded in 2005 by independent bottler Anthony Wills with the aim of reviving the long-lost tradition of farm distilling, using locally cut peat to malt the barley (much of it actually grown on the farm) in Kilchoman's own traditional floor maltings.

It was the first new venture on Islay for 124 years, and the first three-year-old spirit was released in late 2009; in 2011 the first bottling of all-Islay malt arrived. All its output has won rave reviews and most bottlings have sold out almost immediately.

Kilchoman

It's a small venture and the standard tour doesn't take all that long. But the experience is well worth the fairly hairy eight-mile drive from Bowmore: The distillery itself is functional rather than pretty but the setting is suitably rugged, with low rocky crags all around and the sea within earshot; the visitor facilities are extremely smart; and it's a rare opportunity for the tourist to see all the processes from grain to bottle on one compact and easily intelligible site.

Cafe, shop, visitor center. Two tours daily Monday through Friday winter, Monday through Saturday summer. Extended tours Wednesday afternoons. Ring to book.

■ *Lagavulin*

Port Ellen, PA42 7DZ. 01496 302749
discovering-distilleries.com

Lagavulin's low white-painted distillery, set on the south coast with the hills of County Antrim 20 miles away plainly visible on a clear day and in the shadow of Dunnyvaig Castle's stark ruins, seems almost too humble to be the home of such an aristocrat of malt. But for some connoisseurs Lagavulin, especially at 60 years old, is the perfect expression of Islay malt—as peaty as Laphroaig but fuller in body—and is the heart of the world-famous White Horse blend.

The distillery was licensed in 1816 by the landowner, James Johnston, reputedly the descendant of generations of moonshiners. For

Lagavulin, especially at 60 years old, is the perfect expression of Islay malt—as peaty as Laphroaig but fuller in body—and is the heart of the world-famous White Horse blend.

a while it had a neighbor, Ardmore, licensed in 1817, but it wasn't long before the two were merged and modernized. In the 1860s it was taken over by Mackie's of Glasgow, which owned a number of distilleries on the mainland. Sir Peter Mackie not only created White Horse, he also, in 1908, opened a small craft distillery on the site which functioned until 1962.

Lagavulin became part of the Distillers Company combine in 1927 and is now one of Diageo's flagship distilleries and, indeed, one of its flagship single malts.

Shop. Standard tours: five per day, seven days winter, seven per day Monday through Friday summer. Warehouse Demonstrations Monday through Friday, 10:30 am. Tastings Monday through Friday, 1:30 pm. Ring to book.

Laphroaig

■ *Laphroaig*
Port Ellen, PA42 7DU. 01496 302418
laphroaig.com

Of all the widely available Islay malts, Laphroaig has long been regarded as the peatiest. For many it's an acquired taste that marks out the true connoisseur; for just as many others, its near-medicinal tang has been too high a hurdle (although as a plus, its iodine flavor persuaded the US authorities during Prohibition that it really was a medicine and could therefore be prescribed as such). But love it or hate it, this Marmite of a malt has long been a world-class performer.

Laphroaig was founded at the same time as Lagavulin just up the coast, and also by a family named Johnston. While Lagavulin was sold to Mackie's, though, Laphroaig remained in family hands. A bitter feud between the neighbors over a trading agreement culminated in 1907 when Peter Mackie blocked Laphroaig's water supply; the matter was resolved in court but they like to say at Laphroaig that Mackie's craft distillery was an attempt to replicate and undercut their distinctive product.

The last of the Johnstons died in 1954 and left the whole shooting match to his secretary, Bessie Williamson, who reigned until 1972. She then sold the company to Long John International, part of Whitbread, and since then it has changed ownership many times, ending up in the hands of the Jim Beam group. But such is its reputation that none of its corporate owners has ever given in to the urge to tone down its peatiness in the search for wider acceptance. Nor have they even sought to cut costs by closing the distillery's traditional floor maltings.

Shop and visitor center. Two tours per day winter, four in summer. Daily tastings. Water to Whisky experience every weekday in summer: Walk to water source, drive to peat banks, return to distillery. Ring to book.

■ *Isle of Jura*

Craighouse, PA60 7XT. 01496 820385
isleofjura.com

There's much debate among whisky fanciers as to whether Isle of Jura should be classified with the peaty malts of its nearest neighbor, Islay, or with the gentler liquors of the Highlands. Jura has peat, to be sure, but in ancient times the island was covered with birchwood, unlike Islay, so the composition of the peat is different and the flavors it confers are less pungent.

Be that as it may, the islanders have supposedly been distilling whisky illegally since the 16th century, and in 1810 or thereabouts the Laird, Archibald Campbell, decided to go legit. Various tenants ran the enterprise over the years, and in 1876 the operator, James Ferguson, expanded its capacity and rebuilt it, according to one visitor, as "one of the handsomest we have seen, and from the bay it looks more like a castle than a distillery." Unfortunately, in 1901 Ferguson and the Laird, Colin Campbell, fell out over the rent: Ferguson did a moonlight flit and took the equipment with him.

Thus it remained until 1960, when to boost the island's faltering economy landowners Tony Riley-Smith of Ardfin and Robin Fletcher of Ardlussa enlisted the help of MacKinlay's and its renowned designer, William Delme-Evans (a Welshman!), to install a new distillery in the shell of the old. Since then it has gone from strength to strength, supplying the malt component for blends including Whyte & Mackay (whose parent company now owns it) and achieving wide distribution and recognition for its own bottlings.

Shop. Tours twice a day Monday through Friday (summer), once a day (winter). Ring to book.

In 1960, to boost the island's economy, a Welsh designer, William Delme-Evans was commissioned to install a new distillery in the shell of the old at the Isle of Jura.

Oban *including Mull*

When Dr. Johnson and his faithful sidekick Boswell passed through Oban in 1773 they found "a tolerable inn" but not much else: The place then was a scatter of fishermen's and boatbuilders' cottages huddled beneath the towering walls of **Dunollie Castle**, a formidable stronghold dating back to the Pictish kingdom of Dalriada in the 7th or 8th century and since medieval times a seat of the mighty Clan MacDougall. There was also a small trading station exporting local produce via the almost perfect harbor—a west-facing semicircular bay protected by the island of Kerrera.

Only four years after Dr. Johnson's visit a pair of entrepreneurial local landowners, the brothers John and Hugh Stevenson, started a new shipping business in Oban's near-perfect harbor, dealing mostly in granite from the area's excellent quarries and hardwood from its untapped forests. It was exactly the right time to be in the building supplies trade: Scotland was being urbanized at a rate almost unequalled in modern history, with new towns going up in Edinburgh and the other major centers and planned villages and townships sprouting all over the map as "improving" landlords sought both to impose order on their tenants and maximize the income from their estates. Oban grew and thrived and in 1811 was chartered as a burgh.

Tourism rather than trade, though, was the driving force behind Oban's Victorian expansion and prosperity. The visitors followed in the footsteps of Sir Walter Scott, who paused here in 1814 and admired its "romantic prospect;" after that the area to the north of the old town started filling up with substantial, in some cases even palatial villas, many of which are today hotels. One project that failed, though, was an ambitious plan to build a giant "hydropathic sanatorium" above the town. The investors ran out of money in 1881, just after the arrival of the railway which, if they had been able to hold on a little longer, would surely have kept all 137 bedrooms nicely filled. The roof was never put on and the walls eventually crumbled into dereliction.

The roof never went on to **McCaig's Tower**, either, but the walls still dominate the town. The structure, designed to look like the Colosseum in Rome, was started in 1897 by a local banker and philanthropist, John McCaig, as an art gallery and museum. When he died in 1902 his family decided to enjoy the remnants of his fortune rather than squander it on benefactions: The unfinished "tower" is now a public garden.

Tourism is still the driving force of Oban's economy: During the season visitors comfortably outnumber the town's 8,000 residents. Some are only passing through, as the harbor is CalMac's busiest terminal with services to Lismore, Mull, Coll, Tiree, Colonsay, and Barra. For those who stay, the town's attractions include not one but two cathedrals—the **Roman Catholic cathedral** designed by Giles Gilbert Scott, and the **Scottish Episcopalian St. John the Divine** started in 1863 and still not exactly finished. **The Museum of War & Peace** commemorates Oban's role in World War II when it was an important naval base during the Battle of the Atlantic, with several surrounding airfields including one where long-range flying boats were based. The neighboring beaches were used for D-Day training; and during the Cold War, Gallanach Bay was linked to Newfoundland by the first underwater telephone cable, TAT 1, which carried the hotline between the White House and the Kremlin. Nearby are **Dunstaffnage Castle**, the mainland base of the MacDougall Lords of the Isles; the **Scottish Sealife Centre** at Barcaldine on Loch Creran; and the gardens of the medieval **Ardchattan Priory**.

Eating and drinking can be a memorable experience in Oban. It has never hosted one of Scotland's biggest fishing fleets, but what it lacks in quantity it makes up for in quality. The superb produce, especially shellfish, of the surrounding waters is the specialty of many restaurants in the town dubbed the Seafood Capital of Scotland. There are other treats as well: The **Cuan Mor** in George Street is home to the **Oban Bay Brewery**, but its bar overlooking the bay also stocks 100 single malts, and in Markie Dan's bar at the **Corran House** on Corran Esplanade you'll find another 100. There's a branch of **The Whisky Shop**, too, right by the railway station.

Mull, less than an hour's ferry ride from Oban, is the second largest of the Inner Hebrides, and with a resident population of fewer than 3,000 it's hardly the most crowded place on earth! To make it emptier still, much of the central part of the island is extremely mountainous—**Ben More** is the highest peak at 3,169 feet—which leaves plenty of space for wildlife. And the speciality here is eagles: Not just golden eagles, but also rare white-tailed sea eagles, which were introduced from the neighboring isle of Rum in 2005 and have established a stable breeding population.

It goes without saying that a holiday on Mull is likely to be of the rugged outdoors variety: Hill-walking, bird-spotting, and whale-watching are among the most popular activities, although there's also golf for those who prefer a gentler pursuit, as well as many sandy beaches on which to laze in the mild summer weather—August temperatures tend to peak at about 18°C (64°F).

But there's another speciality here, too—Christianity. A mile off the southwestern tip of Mull lies the tiny island of **Iona**, where the Irish Saint Columba established his monastery in 563 CE. It quickly became the headquarters of the Celtic church and maintained its sway for a century until the Synod of Whitby in 664 CE at which the Celts gave way to the Roman church. Iona's loss of supremacy was compounded by a series of hugely destructive Viking raids (during which the Book of Kells was spirited away to Ireland for safety). Once the Norse invaders had evolved from pirates into settlers it regained much of its earlier importance: Among the Scottish kings who chose to be buried here are Duncan, his slayer Macbeth, and his slayer in turn, Malcolm. (The Labour leader John Smith, who is not known to have slain anyone, also chose to be buried here.) The abbey church has been an ecumenical center since 1934. The 50-mile scenic drive from Mull's capital, Tobermory, takes you to the foot-ferry at Fionnphort—no visitors' cars are allowed on Iona, but then Iona is so small as to be easily toured by bike or boot.

Another island to visit is **Staffa**, site of **Fingal's cave**—a sea-cave of hexagonal basalt pillars identical to the Giant's Causeway in Northern Ireland, but much taller. The cave is 65 ft from sea-level to ceiling and has inspired poets, painters, and musicians including Tennyson, Turner, and Mendelssohn. In fact there's a **Mendelssohn on Mull Festival** every July at which young professional musicians perform his and other composers' works in various venues around the island. Music with a more local flavour can be enjoyed at the island's music festival in April, when folk artists play at pubs around the island, and the **Fiddlers' Rally** in September at the Aros Centre in Tobermory.

If all seems peaceful and civilized now, Mull still has a bloody history. The Macleans and the Campbells were rivals for dominance and permanently at each others' throats. Legend has it that the soldiers aboard a troop-transport of the Spanish Armada, wrecked here in 1588, were conscripted as mercenaries by Lachlan Mor Maclean of Duart Castle; in 1647 during the Civil War the Macleans were Royalists, and the castle beat off a Campbell siege only to fall six years later to Cromwell's navy. Duart was demolished by the Campbells in 1691, but the Macleans had the last laugh: The ruins were bought in 1911 by Sir Fitzroy Donald Maclean, who then built the comfortable Scottish baronial country house you may visit today.

Tobermory's main street includes a number of pubs and restaurants, of which **MacGochan's** towards the southern end is recommended for its seafood, choice of real ales, and selection of single malts.

■ *Ardnamurchan*

Glenbeg PH36 4JG. 01972 500285
ardnamurchan@adelphidistillery.com

If ever a distillery was designed to attract the whisky-loving tourist, Ardnamurchan is it. And that's despite the fact that as the most westerly distillery on the Scottish mainland, it's miles from anywhere and, frankly, a bit of a swine to get to.

Ardnamurchan was opened in 2014 by the Adelphi Distillery, which is not a distillery at all but a very high-end independent bottler. It *was* a distillery once—in fact it was the largest grain distillery in Scotland until 1932, when it was mothballed by the Distillers Company. It was demolished in 1970, and in 1983 the astonishingly beautiful Glasgow Central Mosque was built on the site. The name was revived in 1993 by Jamie Walker, great-grandson of the Archibald Walker who owned Adelphi from 1880–1906, and in 2007 the company started the planning and preparatory work on Ardnamurchan.

The new distillery was formally declared open by Princess Anne on July 25th 2014, and despite (or perhaps because of) its remote-

Ardnamurchan; photo ©Mark Armin Giesler

ness it is proving a popular destination. Perhaps one reason for that is that it's only the latest of the many attractions on the Ardnamurchan Estate on the shore of Loch Sunart, along with the nature trails, outdoor sports, and activities, and the delightful Glenborrodale Castle. The estate and surrounding holiday parks also offer a range of accommodation from campsites to holiday cottages. The distillery itself is entirely newly built, but to a traditional design, and prides itself on its environmentally friendly energy hydroelectric power and woodchip boilers.

The easiest way to get to Ardnamurchan is to take the ferry from Tobermory on Mull to Kilchoan; the estate is about 10 rather windy miles along the single-track B8007, so allow a good 1½ hours for the trip. If you're not starting from Mull, you head south along the A82 from Fort William, and after nine miles hop on the little ferry across Loch Lynne at Inchree to Corran; then it's a slow but scenic 25-mile drive along the A861 to Salen, and then on to the B8007 for even slower but equally scenic 12 miles to Glenbeg.

Visitor center; opening times vary according to season, so always ring ahead. Basic tour £7; premium tour £12; connoisseur's tour £25; manager's tour £40. Connoisseur's and manager's tours must be booked in advance.

■ *Ben Nevis*

Lochy Bridge, Fort William PH33 6TJ. 01397 700200
bennevisdistillery.com

Directly beneath the frowning brow of Ben Nevis stands the eponymous distillery. The rugged grandeur of the surrounding mountains makes Fort William the tourist trap that it is; but it's not a trait you'll find echoed in the distillery visitor center, the star of whose audio-visual presentation is the mythical (make that fictional) Scottish giant Hector McDram.

Quite why a giant needs to be invented when Ben Nevis was founded in 1825 by a real one—Long John MacDonald, whose 6′ 4″ may not be that impressive to the modern eye but certainly was to his contemporaries—is a question for the distillery's Japanese owners, Asahi Breweries.

Long John's heirs were successful not only at making but also at branding their whisky: Bottled as Dew of Ben Nevis, it sold well enough to require the building in 1878 of a completely new distillery, Glen Nevis, next door to the original. Glen Nevis functioned as a separate entity for 30 years, when the two plants were integrated. In 1906 the MacDonalds launched the blend named after the founder, which they sold in 1911 to a London wine and spirit merchant,

Ben Nevis

Chaplin's. In due course the whisky became more famous than its native distillery and Seager Evans, which bought Chaplin's in 1936, changed its own name to Long John International. And in 1981, to complete the cycle, Long John International bought Ben Nevis. So what goes around, in this case, really does come around. (Although it doesn't then stop: Ben Nevis was sold on to Asahi in 1989.)

The distillery, which stands on the A82 two miles out of Fort William, just past the junction with the A830, is not particularly attractive to look at following extensive alterations by Joseph Hobbs, the Canadian entrepreneur who owned it from 1955–1964. The setting, though, is undeniably magnificent and visitor center, fancifully titled "The Legend of the Dew," carved out of the old bottling hall and a Victorian warehouse in 1991 is smart and up-to-date if a little over-commercial for some tastes.

Visitor centre. Shop. Cafe/restaurant. Open Monday through Friday 9 am to 5 pm, year round, Saturday 10 am to 4 pm, Easter through September; Sunday 12 noon to 6 pm, July through August.

■ *Oban*

Stafford Street, Oban PA34 5NH. 01631 572004
discovering-distilleries.com

One of Diageo's smallest distilleries, Oban stands on such a cramped site in the very center of town that when they wanted new warehousing in the 1890s they had to dig backwards into the cliff. That's when the workmen broke through into a cave containing eight Mesolithic skeletons, four adults and four children.

By that time the distillery was already nearly a century old, having been founded in 1793 as a brewery by the Stevenson brothers. A certain amount of distilling seems to have been carried out, on and off, in those early years despite competition from the moonshiners in the surrounding hills, but it wasn't until the 1820s that whisky took over from beer as the site's principal product. The fourth generation of the Stevenson family, Thomas, was in charge for 32 years from 1829 (the first three generations seemed to have had little staying-power!) and secured Oban's reputation as a fine small-still whisky, but sold up after the death of his son and heir.

After a regular pass-the-parcel of ownership changes during the alternating booms and busts of the 1870s to the 1930s, Oban ended

Oban; photo ©Angus Bremner

up in the hands of The Distillers Company, now Diageo, which set the seal on the 14-year-old's quality by including it in the original Classic Malts line-up of 1988. It also opened the doors to the public, and despite the squash, the Sensory & Flavour Finding tour was soon attracting 35,000 visitors a year. There's also a more luxurious Exclusive Distillery Tour offering comparative tastings of different bottlings.

Shop. Check website for opening times. Last tour 1 hour 15 minutes before closing. Exclusive Distillery Tour should be booked in advance. Groups should also book.

■ *Tobermory*
Tobermory PA75 6NR. 01688 302647
tobermorymalt.com

British visitors know the name Tobermory from the children's TV series "The Wombles," one of which was named after the town. They will also recognize the town's brightly painted seafront from another children's TV series, "Ballamory." Tobermory's distillery, though, is strictly for grown-ups.

The township was founded in 1788 by the British Fisheries Society as one of 50 projected villages intended to improve the herring fisheries in the west of Scotland. In the event only three were built, as they failed to attract crofters into the industry. Tobermory's

Tobermory; photo ©ralphdunning

distillery, founded 10 years later, provided employment for the failed fishermen and was a respectable, tax-paying alternative to moonshining.

At first known as Ledaig, it survived until 1837 when the clearances slashed the local population from 10,000 to 3,000, but was reopened in 1878—only to close again in 1930. After that it was used variously as a worker's canteen and a power station until 1972, when it was reopened again. It was very touch and go, though, opening and closing several times—among the failed owners was a West Yorkshire property company—until 1993 when it was bought by the substantial independent distiller Burn Stewart which also owns Deanston and Bunnahabhain and is now a subsidiary of South African wines and spirits giant Distell.

Since then it has thrived, the distinctive squat green Tobermory bottle becoming a familiar sight on supermarket shelves. Burn Stewart has also gone back to the Ledaig name for a heavily peated malt in keeping with local tradition.

Open 10 am to 5 pm Monday through Friday. Tours must be booked ahead.

Western Isles

Thirty years ago Skye was an ailing agricultural backwater dominated by crafting and soft fruit growing supplemented by an underdeveloped tourist trade. Today it has turned itself into a tourist paradise, mainly by exploiting its spectacular and hugely varied scenery.

Skye has much in common with the surrounding islands—prehistoric monuments aplenty, Viking heritage, abundant wildlife, grand castles of the clan chieftains, and a population diminished by the clearances from 23,000, 150 years ago to 9,000 today. But it's Skye's spectacularly rugged scenery that sets it apart. From the twin ranges of the Black and Red Cuillins (the highest point being Sgurr Alasdair at 3,255 ft) in the west of the island, four great peninsulas reach out, each one being geologically very different. Ancient volcanoes and more recent glaciers have left jagged peaks that only experienced mountaineers can climb, towering stacks such as the Quiraing and the Old Man of Storr, dizzying sea-cliffs, the double rock arch of Ardmore Point, thundering waterfalls, a coral beach at Claigan, secluded glacial lochs, and tiny rocky offshore islets crowded with seabirds.

The scenery has always been there, of course; and some of the more traditional attractions such as **Dunvegan Castle**, seat of the chiefs of the MacLeods, with its ornamental gardens and the Fairy Flag under which the clan went into battle, have been around for quite a while too. But in recent decades—and perhaps prompted by the fact that Skye is the most accessible of the Hebrides—the entrepreneurs of tourism have been adding more and more activities to the island's repertoire. At sea there's whale-watching (which includes basking sharks, now that the northern seas are warming, as well as seals, dolphins, porpoises, orcas, minke whales, and other cetaceans), kayaking, scuba diving, sailing (anything from dinghies to yachts), and of course windsurfing. On land there's climbing (all grades from the elementary to the terrifying), hiking and rambling (ditto), riding and trekking, mountain biking, sand yachting, archery, falconry, and gulley-running.

The less physical visitor might be more attracted by museums and activity centers such as the **Museum of Island Life** at Kilmuir, the **Toy Museum** at Glendale, and the **Clan Donald Centre** at Armadale Castle, and also by the work of the many craftspeople and artists to whom Skye is now home. Then there's traditional music, which has undergone a considerable renaissance in the last 30 years. This has included the revival of the clarsach, or Celtic harp, and the reintroduction of the local traditional style of fiddle-playing, which was brought back to its old home (having been effectively banned by the kirk a century ago) by the Canadian descendants of the victims of the clearances. The annual fortnight-long Skye Festival hasn't been held since 2009, alas, but instead there are regular recitals, ceilidhs, and general knees-ups at various venues throughout the year.

The icing on the cake is the food and drink. As elsewhere in the west of Scotland, the pubs and restaurants of Skye have started making the most of the region's produce which here includes not only locally raised meat and freshly caught fish and seafood, but also Skye-grown soft fruit, Skye-made cheeses, Skye-brewed beer, and of course Skye's own whisky. There are many, many establishments to choose from, but with its superb restaurant, its 400-odd whiskies, its own brewery on site, and its spectacular setting between the foot of the Cuillins and the head of a long sealoch, the **Sligachan Hotel** on the A87 a few miles south of Portree is a must-visit. The fact that it's the *Good Pub Guide's* whisky pub of the year for 2013, 2015, and 2016 is an added incentive. You might also try the **Stein Inn** on Vaternish near Dunvegan on Skye's north coast, whose 125 malts make the slightly hairy trip along the B886 well worthwhile. And for something to take home, call in at Isle Ornsay or Eilean Iarman on the south coast where independent and heavily Gaelic-accented blender **Praban na Linne Ltd.'s** shop will sell you its blended malt Poit Dubh, its peaty blend Te Bheag, and its lighter blend Mac na Mara.

Lewis, the northern half of the largest of the Hebrides, has always suffered—at least, as far as tourism is concerned—from its remoteness: The ferry at Ullapool is a fairly testing 225-mile drive from Glasgow, and takes over 2.5 hours. It is, however, much closer to Skye: The crossing from Uig (15 miles up the A87 from Portree) to Tarbert takes just over an hour in good weather.

Lewis doesn't have the spectacular scenery of Orkney or Skye—its highest point, Mealisval, is 1,833 ft, and there aren't the skerries, stacks, and sea-cliffs that closer islands can boast—while the historical attractions, the stone circles, the brochs, the Iron Age remains, aren't as profuse as those on Skye nor as well-preserved as, say, Skarra Brae (although the Viking chess set discovered in 1831 has become an international icon, and the stone circle at Callanish is not known as the Stonehenge of the Hebrides without reason).

Not that Lewis doesn't have its unique attractions: The Harris tweed industry, despite the name, is now concentrated here, with finishing mills at the capital, Stornoway, and Shawbost and Carloway on the Atlantic coast. But Lewis's real strong point is its emptiness. Its 683 square miles supports a population of just 18,000, 12,000 of whom live in and around Stornoway. The rest are concentrated on the east coast and the northern tip of the island, so the interior is the wanderer's paradise, especially noted for its innumerable freshwater lochs. It seems the rare chance of solitude is not without its admirers, either: Tourism has been creeping upwards and is now worth over £45 million a year to the island's economy. The three-day **Hebridean Celtic Festival**, held in the grounds of Stornoway Castle every July, is a particular draw, attracting crowds of up to 10,000.

The emptiness is accounted for by the clearances of the mid-19th century, the subsequent famine, and the conversion of much of the arable to sheep and sporting estates by absentee landlords which entailed yet more wholesale evictions. These landlords, notably the English industrialists Sir James Matheson and Lord Leverhulme, invested heavily in industrial projects such as a fish cannery at Stornoway; but nothing could replace the crofting which had been the island's mainstay.

Depopulation also had its effect on Lewis's distilling tradition: There was a legal distillery, Shoeburn, in Stornoway in the 1830s, and one or two other attempts before that; but other than that the field has been left to moonshiners whose activities were constrained more by the island's very strong Presbyterianism than by Her Majesty's Customs & Excise. There's a strong rumor that illegal distilling has persisted much longer in Lewis's empty and trackless interior than in more densely populated regions, so if you find yourself wandering the watery wilderness of South Lewis, watch out for wisps of smoke!

Harris, the southern portion of the island, has the highest mountain in the Outer Hebrides—The Clisham at 2,621 ft—but other than that is, like Lewis, fairly flat. Its population numbers just 2,000, of whom 600 live in Tarbert and the rest mainly in South Harris. South Harris is particularly known for its beaches of white sand.

■ Abhainn Dearg

Carnish, Lewis HS2 9EX. 01851 672429
abhainndearg.co.uk

One of the pioneers of Scotland's new generation of artisanal craft distilleries, Abhainn Dearg is also its most westerly and probably—although there's no objective measure for this—its most remote.

Situated on the banks of the little river from which it takes its name—and from which it draws its water—Abhainn Dearg is a long but beautiful drive from Stornaway along the A858 to Garrynahine, then on to the B8011, and then along a little unclassified road from Timsgearraidh. And it's well worth the trip, not just to see the distillery itself. As a collection of battered sheds that used to be a fish hatchery it's hardly easy on the eye, despite the giant replicas of the famous Viking-era Lewis chessman that line the drive. No, what you'll see here is an idea in action.

Lewis man Mark Tayburn conceived the project not just as a way of reviving the art of distilling on the island, but as something much more rounded. He grows his own barley—something that hasn't been done here for generations; he raises Highland cattle to eat the spent grain; and he plans to open his own maltings to complete the cycle. He fertilizes the barley with seaweed from the beach nearby, uses the river to power his own hydro-electric plant, and plants a new oak sapling for every cask he uses. And although new, Abhainn Dearg has already grown roots in the community: One day an unknown local left a small pot-still at the door. It had been used... but not legally. Now it is in use again occasionally, but this time legally; and the oddly shaped, much bigger wash and spirit stills you see are scaled-up versions of the traditional one. In another nod to tradition, Mark uses old-fashioned worm-tub condensers.

Mark Tayburn conceived the project [Abhainn Dearg]not just as a way of reviving the art of distilling on the island, but as something much more rounded. He grows his own barley... he raises Highland cattle to eat the spent grain; and he plans to open his own maltings to complete the cycle.

Mark opened the distillery in 2008, launched an immature new make, Spirit of Lewis, in 2010, and released his first limited edition of three-year-old single malt—the youngest age at which it can be bottled as whisky—at the Royal National Mod (Scotland's eisteddfod) when it was held in Stornoway in 2011. Part of his mission is to explain, so although there is no fancy visitor center-cum-shop-cum-restaurant at Abhainn Dearg, he will be delighted to show you round in person. And if you want a more in-depth experience, he also runs a three-day whisky school.

Open 10:30 am to 1 pm, and 2 pm to 3:30 pm, Monday through Friday. Parties ring ahead.

Isle of Harris

■ *Isle of Harris*
Tarbert, Harris HS3 3DJ. 01859 502212
info@harrisdistillery.com

Although a privately owned and fully commercial venture, Isle of Harris calls itself "the social distillery" and was conceived as an enterprise that would benefit and draw together the whole community, not only creating jobs where jobs are sorely needed but bringing Harris's special qualities to the attention of the world. Which implies, of course, a very warm welcome for visitors from far-flung places.

Founder and chairman Anderson Bakewell is an American-born musicologist and organic farmer whose connection with Harris goes back four decades—he owns the island of Scarp, 15 miles up the coast from Tarbert and uninhabited since 1971. He and managing director Simon Erlanger—an executive director of Glenmorangie for 15 years, and one of the team that brought Ardbeg on Islay back into full production—raised £10 million in grants, loans, and investments to open the purpose-built distillery on Tarbert's harborfront in September 2015. It's equipped with two small stills custom-made by an old-established Italian firm of coppersmiths, Frilli of Monterrigioni near Siena: The gin still, nicknamed The Dottach, was first into action with Isle of Harris gin made with locally gathered botanicals; the spirit still, nicknamed Eva, produced its first new make in December 2015 and a bottling is expected, if all goes according to plan, in 2019.

Although tourists are more than welcome to Isle of Harris, they won't find an all-singing all-dancing visitor center with cafe and restaurant serving locally caught seafood gussied up to cordon bleu standard. It's all a bit cozier than that: There's a peat fire always burning in the grate in the still room; there's a shop that sells all manner of local produce including essential oils and cosmetics from Amanda Saurin, who also gathers the botanicals for the gin; and there's a staff canteen where the 10 distillery workers take their lunch and where you, as their honored guest, are welcome to take yours too.

Shop and canteen open Monday through Saturday year round. Tours £10, book ahead.

■ *Talisker*

Carbost, IV47 8SR. 01478 614 308
discovering-distilleries.com

Skye's only distillery is not actually in the eponymous village but is on the shore of Loch Harport near Carbost. (And make sure you get the right Carbost: Not the one four miles north of Portree on the A87, but the one 12 miles southwest of Portree on the B885 and A863.)

After the scenic drive from Portree the distillery itself is something of a disappointment: Most of the severely functional complex is less than 50 years old, having been largely rebuilt after a major fire in 1960: Certainly you would never guess by looking that the

Talisker; photo ©Angus Bremner

distillery has been here since 1830. The location, though, on the shore of a sea loch surrounded by the jagged peaks of the Cuillins, is truly magnificent.

Talisker is one of the true aristocrats of single malts and wins award after award. Its early years were somewhat checkered, though: The local minister thundered against it as "one of the greatest curses that could befall;" the laird wouldn't allow a pier to be built until 1900, so casks had to be floated out to waiting ships (some didn't make it!); and several of the earliest owners went bust. Only when phylloxera caused a worldwide shortage of Cognac was Talisker's quality generally recognized: Today it is a consistent world-beater—and the distillery itself is extremely visitor-friendly.

Shop. Tours Monday through Friday, November through February; closed March; Monday through Saturday, April through May and October; 7 days June through September. Phone ahead to check availability. Groups must book.

Northern Isles *including Caithness*

The 70-odd islands that make up the Orkneys range from quite large to extremely small, lie a mere six miles off the northeast tip of Scotland, and are, it has to be confessed, absolutely fabulous. You could spend a year exploring and not run out of things to see and do. And the islands' attractions and delights are so varied that there's something for almost everyone.

Perhaps the best-known sites are also the oldest—**Skarra Brae** stone-age village, not only built but even furnished with stone slabs, all miraculously preserved by encroaching sand; **Maeshowe** chambered tomb; the **Ring of Brodgar** stone circle. The three together comprise a World Heritage Site but are only a tiny fraction of the prehistoric remains that stud the islands. For despite its latitude, Orkney is extremely rich farmland. The climate is mild and even, thanks to the Gulf Steam; the topography is low, rounded, and easy to plough; and the soil is both fertile and friable. As the ice age receded, people returned in numbers first as wandering bands of hunter-gatherers, then from about 6,000 BCE as settlers and farmers. The Picts succeeded the earliest peoples; the Vikings conquered the Picts; the Scottish kings mastered the Vikings. To all these successive rulers Orkney and its surrounding seas were a very wealthy province, and they have all left their mark—not just the Stone Age relics, but Iron forts, Pictish brochs, the magnificent **Viking cathedral of St. Magnus** in Kirkwall, and the renaissance palace of the Stewart earls.

At the heart of the islands is **Scapa Flow**, one of the biggest and finest natural harbors in the Northern hemisphere and the Royal Navy home fleet's base in both world wars. Vast numbers of men were stationed here, and despite the apparent security of the harbor many ships sank in it: The entire German High Seas Fleet scuttled itself here in 1919 rather than surrender, and many wrecks are still visible and can be explored by divers. In October 1939 a U-boat slipped through the defenses and torpedoed the obsolete battleship Royal Oak with the loss of 833 lives; as a result Churchill ordered

You can scarcely move in Orkney for pubs, hotel bars, and restaurants with decent selections of whisky

the building of the barriers that bear his name and today provide causeways for the A961 Kirkwall-Ronaldsay road. All over Orkney there are gun emplacements, rocket batteries, dug-outs and other wartime sites to be explored.

More recently, and as complete contrast, Orkney has become a haven, almost a colony, for artists and craftspeople producing jewelry, pottery, tapestry and embroidery, and all other wares imaginable. It's also the scene of almost year-round arts and other festivals—folk in May, fine wine in June, **St. Magnus Arts** at midsummer, **Stromness Shopping Week** (not quite as it sounds!) in July, science in September. Most, apart from the last, involve plenty of music and dancing.

Another contrast is provided by the juxtaposition of well-mannered farmland, populated by sheep and beef cattle and growing prodigious amounts of barley and potatoes, and unspoiled wilderness. Orkney is rich in wildlife, and not just seabirds such as gannets, skuas, and puffins, but also grey and common seal, dolphins, porpoises, and orcas. The Royal Society for the Protection of Birds (RSPB) has 20,000 acres of reserves scattered across the islands. The dedicated walker could spend a lifetime roaming these islands, returning to their hotel each evening for some of the finest locally produced beef, lamb, seafood, beer, and malt whisky in the entire country.

Being populous and fertile, Orkney has always had both the ingredients and the demand for whisky. But in the turbulent 18th century its distillers—like those across Scotland—had no appetite for paying duty on what they produced. What seems to have set Orkney apart is the extent to which the moonshiners corrupted public officials who not only turned a blind eye to the smuggling of whisky to the mainland but also, in the case of the Provost of Kirkwall and even the local naval commander, took part in it. The most notorious, Magnus Eunson, was a church beadle. In the early 19th century, though, a number of licensed and legal distilleries were established, one in Kirkwall by a former smuggler named William Traill, another near Stromness which lasted until 1928, and Highland Park.

You can scarcely move in Orkney for pubs, hotel bars, and restaurants with decent selections of whisky, so it's hard to pick any out; but the **Lynnfield Hotel** on Holm Road, Kirkwall—only a few yards from the gates of the Highland Park distillery—carries more than 200 and has a restaurant that specializes in seaweed-fed Holmy lamb. The **Stromness Hotel** in Stromness, which is wonderfully located for the **UNESCO Heart of Neolithic Orkney World Heritage Site**, has more than 100 malts and ale from the Orkney Brewery. For take-home shopping, **John Scott & Miller Ltd.** in Bridge Street, Kirkwall, is one of the quirkiest stores you're likely to encounter. It started life in the late 19th century as a general grocer and wine merchant, then expanded into hardware and giftware. Gradually the grocery side of the business fell away, so now it's a hardware and gift store—but still with a selection of more than 50 rare malts from independent merchants, including its very own bottlings of Highland Park and Scapa.

Wick, home of Old Pulteney (which was the mainland's most northerly Scotch distillery until the opening of Wolfburn at Thurso on the northern coast) is included here rather than among mainland itineraries because while it's a rather wiggly 70-mile drive from Tain (see below), it's only a 25-minute flight from Kirkwall or, if you're driving, 21 miles to Scrabster and then a 90-minute ferry-ride to Stromness. It's made up of two distinct halves: The rather higgledy-piggledy streets of Wick proper north of the eponymous river, and more orderly grid of the planned settlement of Pulteneytown to the south. The town is known for its artificial harbor, designed by Thomas Telford and once the biggest herring fishery in the world, and for its ruined castles—not one, not two, but three, as mementoes of even harsher times.

Whisky tourists arriving by train are in luck: just three minutes' walk from the station, in Union Street, is **Mackay's Hotel**, whose impressive range of limited editions and special bottlings includes No. 1 Ebenezer Place. This is the hotel's formal postal address, and it's unique—and not just in the way that all postal addresses are unique. There is no No. 2 Ebenezer Place.

...[Highland Park] has its own floor-maltings and its own turbary at Hobbister Moor seven miles away; it can still therefore produce 20% of its own malt.

■ *Highland Park*

Holm Rd., Kirkwall KW15 1SU. 01856 874619
highlandpark.co.uk

Scotland's most northerly distillery is also one of the oldest, having been founded in 1798 by David Robertson on the very site of the bothie once occupied by the notorious smuggler and churchman Magnus Eunson. A nicely symbolic location, this, since the history of whisky in the late 18th-early 19th centuries concerns the struggle of legitimate commercial distillers and their allies in customs to suppress illicit small-scale distilling and smuggling.

Highland Park was a well-kept secret until 1979. Orkney had fewer tourists, and very little of the mildly peated product was released to merchants for independent bottling. Connoisseurs (including Winston Churchill) praised it; but other than that its honeyed, heathery delights were known only to the blenders who prized it so highly. In that year, however, it "came out" as a widely available distillery bottling and soon became one of the most popular single malts in the world.

Much of its character comes from a determined adherence to tradition: It has its own floor-maltings and its own turbary at Hobbister Moor seven miles away; it can still therefore produce 20% of its own malt. The whisky is aged in sherry casks for a slight oloroso sweetness and the peat imparts a very faint smokiness.

Don't be put off by the distillery's windswept and, frankly, somewhat forbidding exterior: The visitor center is one of the most highly regarded in the industry.

Visitors center. Shop. Standard tours on the hour seven days a week (May through August), Monday through Friday (April and September); 2 and 3 pm Monday through Friday (October through March). Phone ahead to book Connoisseur, Viking, and Magnus Eunson tours.

■ *Old Pulteney*

Huddart Street, Pulteneytown, Wick KW1 5BA. 01955 602371
oldpulteney.com

Old Pulteney's very existence is proof of how important whisky was to Scotland's economic development once the 1823 Excise Act had brought the industry under some sort of control. Pulteneytown, on the southern side of the river from the Viking village of Wick,

Old Pulteney

was like Oban: Laid out and built by the local landowner as a way of exploiting the riches of the sea—in this case, herring—both to fatten his own purse and to provide employment for a growing population. It was a huge undertaking, employing no less a civil engineer than Thomas Telford to excavate the harbor and to build a two-mile aqueduct or lade from Loch Hempriggs to the planned distillery.

For the distillery was no afterthought: It provided yet more employment and revenue while keeping bothie-distilled moonshine out of the law-abiding and God-fearing new township. A township, incidentally, which in its early days had no access by road—as with many of the Islay distilleries, everything that came in and went out of Old Pulteney did so by sea.

Wick's herring fishery became a huge business before fading in the early 20th century, but the distillery continued to flourish, outlasting neighbors such as Brabster, Murkle, Greenland, and Gurston which all perished as a result of the 1900 crash. In 1925 it was bought by the Distillers Company, and in 1930 the Depression caught up with it and it was mothballed, only to be bought and reopened in 1951 by R.J. "Bertie" Cumming, also the rescuer of Balblair (see below). He sold it on in 1955, and by the strangest coincidence it was bought 40 years later by Inver House Distillers—the very same company that now operates Balblair!

A peculiarity of Old Pulteney is its stills, which are as short as

Glenmorangie's are tall. The wash still has no swan-neck, the explanation being that the original was too long to fit into the stillhouse, so it was simply cut off, and replacements have been made to the same pattern. An unlikely story—but probably a better one than whatever the truth is.

Visitor center. Shop. Open Monday through Saturday 10 am to 4 pm, May through September; Monday through Friday 10 am to 4 pm, October through April. Tours 11 am and 2 pm, must be booked. Directions: from A99 (Francis Street) turn into Northcote Street; then left into Macrae Street and immediately right into Rutherford Street. The distillery is at the top of the road at the junction with Huddart Street.

■ Scapa

St. Ola, Kirkwall KW15 1SE. 01865 875430
scapamalt.com

Highland Park's lesser-known neighbor only opened its doors to the public in 2015 with the launch of hourly guided tours from April to November. With a staff of only three—even the manager only flies in from Speyside every now and then—it just hadn't been considered feasible to entertain guests, but the continuing growth in whisky tourism must have opened the eyes of owner Chivas Bros to the site's potential.

Built in 1885, Scapa has always been something of a workhorse. Apart from a brief period in mothballs during World War I, when it billeted personnel from the Navy's enormous Scapa Flow base, it chugged along quietly producing fillings for the blenders al-

Scapa

most without interruption except for a brief closure in 1934–1935. In 1959 it was almost completely rebuilt and was equipped with the newly designed Lomond still, a hybrid between a pot still and a continuous still that gives the stillman the ability to make a wide range of styles on the same plant. These were widely used in Hiram Walker-owned distilleries but only two are left, the example here at Scapa and one recently recommissioned at Bruichladdich on Islay.

Scapa was modernized again in 1978 and survived the huge corporate merger of 1988 that created the Allied Distillers empire, only to be mothballed during the recession of the early 1990s. But it soon came back to life, and in 2004 was treated to a £2 million restoration. This was the prelude to its sale to the French-owned Chivas Brothers, which first started bottling Scapa for the first time as a 16-year-old and has now taken the decision to challenge Highland Park for some of the tourist limelight.

Scapa isn't the prettiest distillery in Scotland by a long chalk, but its functional hangar-like buildings enjoy such a spectacular seaside location that a walk along the front actually forms part of the tour!

Hourly tours 9:30 am to 5 pm, seven days a week April to September, 5 days a week October through November. Max 10 per tour. Must book ahead.

Tain

Few towns of its size could make a more delightful or better-provided base for explorations than Tain on the southern shore of Dornoch Firth.

A pretty town in its own right with some interesting buildings (check out the **Tolbooth**, built in the early 18th century as a combined lock-up and muniment room and copying the medieval style of its predecessor), it's proud of a history that goes back to the 11th century and beyond. The district is almost littered with Pictish stones and crosses from the 9th and 10th centuries, and in about 1000 CE Tain was the birthplace of St. Duthac, Bishop of Ross and a great preacher. Duthac died in 1065 CE, and the very next year Tain was made a Royal Burgh by Malcolm III, slayer of Macbeth. Duthac died in Ireland, and his remains weren't brought home for burial until 1253 CE, after which Tain became a noted place of pilgrimage. In 1306 CE, after Robert the Bruce lost the Battle of Methven and was on the run, his wife, daughter, and sisters sought sanctuary in St. Duthac's Chapel here, but were seized by the treacherous Earl of Ross and handed over to the English to suffer many years of harsh imprisonment.

Tain is very conscious of this and other stories from its past: A permanent exhibition in the museum, church, and churchyard, **Tain Through Time,** is well worth a visit. Tain also has a pottery—one of the largest in Scotland, in fact—and **Glasstorm**, a hot glass studio with an international reputation.

The countryside around Tain offers plenty of good walking at all levels from leisurely strolls along its sandy beaches (really!) to more strenuous hikes in the hills and forests inland, with heritage sights to see such as the medieval **Fearn Abbey** and the **Pictish Discovery Centre** at Portmahomack. **Dunrobin Castle** near Clynelish, longtime seat of the mighty Dukes of Sutherland, is open to the public; Skibo Castle, the vast Edwardian Scottish baronial pile built by Andrew Carnegie, is today a very exclusive country club.

But it's the distilleries you've come to see. Glenmorangie is actually in town; Dalmore is 12 miles south on the A9 at Alness, next to Invergordon with its vast grain distillery; Balblair, newly opened to the public, is a mere three miles west of Tain at Edderton on the A836; Clynelish is 19 miles up the coast. And one thing you'll appreciate about Tain as a base is the sheer amount and variety of visitor accommodation from camping and caravan sites through bed and breakfasts and self-catering right up to grand traditional hotels of which Tain—population 3,500!—has not one but three: The amazing Scottish baronial **Mansfield Castle Hotel**, the scarcely less palatial **Morangie House Hotel**, and the quainter-looking but equally elevated **Royal Hotel** in the High Street, with a better than reasonable choice of whiskies in its **Wig & Pen** bar. Try also the **Dornoch Bridge Inn** at Meikle Ferry five minutes away from Tain— recently sold but previously well-known for its range of malts. And whether the Dornoch Bridge under its new owners disappoints or not, make sure that as you travel up the A9 en route to Clynelish you stop at Dornoch, home to the magnificent, splendiferous, and definitely not to be missed **Dornoch Castle Hotel**. This genuine 15th-century crenellated castle has a bar stocked with approaching 300 whiskies, which is impressive enough in itself although not a record. It's the choice of whiskies that counts here: Not just standard bottlings but private bottlings, merchant bottlings, and astonishing rareties from distilleries not merely closed but demolished and built over. And round this collection the hotel has built a program of tutored tastings, blind tastings, competitive tastings and other activities that will make you wish you never had to go home.

■ *Balblair*

Edderton, Tain IV19 1LB. 01862 821273
balblair.com

One of the newer visitor attractions on the malt whisky scene is the multimedia Time Capsule Room at Balblair, just a few miles west of Glenmorangie along the A836 on the southern shore of the Dornoch Firth. And it's fitting that Balblair should have thrown itself open to the public because with a documented foundation date of 1790, it's a contender for the "Scotland's Oldest Distillery" title.

Balblair

Well, that's not entirely true. John Ross definitely started distilling Balblair whisky in 1790, but that was as a sub-tenant of a farmer called Simpson, who was a tenant of the local landowners, the Rosses (possibly related—but then, a lot of people round here are called Ross) of Balnagowan. John Ross became head tenant in 1798 but times were hard—not only was he continually undercut by the moonshiners, he was plagued by bad debt as well. In 1817 he was heavily fined for non-payment of taxes, so the farm remained an important part of the Ross family income. After the 1823 Excise Act tolled the knell of the bothies, though, Balblair prospered and stayed in the Ross family for three generations.

When the last of the Rosses retired in 1894, the tenancy of the now-flourishing distillery went to a Leith wine merchant, Alexander Cowan, who actually rebuilt it beside the railway line two miles from its original site. So the question is: Is this the same Balblair? Whatever your conclusion, it's an undeniably pretty late Victorian distillery, perfect of its type, in as pleasing a setting as you could wish for.

Cowan didn't do so well: Balblair closed in 1911 and remained closed until 1948 when the Blanagowan estate sold the freehold to an entrepreneurial lawyer from Banff, R.J. "Bertie" Cumming. He reopened it, extended it vastly, and sold it on his retirement in 1970 to Hiram Walker. In 1988 Allied Breweries bought it; in 1996 they announced its closure but instead sold it to Inver House Distillers—who have now put all that history on display.

Visitor center. Exhibition. Shop. Tours 11 am and 2 pm, Monday through Friday, must be booked in advance.

Clynelish; photo ©Angus Bremner

■ *Clynelish*

Clynelish Rd, Brora KW9 6LR. 01408 623000
discovering-distilleries.com

As you approach the coastal town of Brora along the A9, you catch sight of the Victorian pagoda of the maltings at the handsome old Clynelish distillery. You also catch sight of the not-so-handsome and much, much bigger new Clynelish distillery.

Clynelish was one of those distilleries founded by improving landlords—in this case the mighty Dukes of Sutherland whose ancestral seat, Dunrobin Castle, is just down the coast—partly to increase the value of their rent-roll, partly to tame their wild moon-shining tenants. It opened in 1819 and was operated by a quick succession of lessees until 1896, when the freehold was bought by Ainslie & Co., blenders and bottlers of Leith, who built an entirely new modern distillery. Until that point the whisky had never been on general release and was only sold to private customers, who raved about it.

Ainslie & Co. was eventually bought by the Distillers Company, which in 1968 opened a second entirely new modern distillery. The original was due to be closed but won a reprieve thanks to a long drought on Islay, where the heavily peated malts used in the Johnnie Walker blend came from. The old Clynelish was dragooned into service to make a very peaty Islay—nothing like the light and spritzy malt for which it had been famous—but needed an identity of its own and therefore operated as Brora until the axe finally fell in 1983. The old buildings, though, survive as warehouses for the new Clynelish—and this being a very big distillery, it needs plenty of space in which to mature its stocks. The "new" Clynelish malt maintains a high reputation and is one of Diageo's Classic Malts range, while visitor numbers at the distillery grow year by year.

Visitor center. Shop. Distillery Tour, Taste of Clynelish Tour, Taste of the Highlands Tour available year-round. See website for opening times.

■ *Dalmore*

Alness IV17 0UT. 01349 882362
thedalmore.com

A cluster of dignified grey stone buildings on the water's edge on the northern shore of the Firth of Cromarty, Dalmore has to rank high among the most picturesque distilleries in Scotland. It's in pleasing contrast to its Whyte & Mackay stablemate a couple of miles along the B817, the Invergordon distillery: Invergordon is a massive factory turning out oceanic quantities of grain whisky, and it seems only right that while an unabashed ethanol factory should look like what it is, a 170-year-old malt whisky distillery should be fit to feature on the lid of a shortbread biscuit tin.

Dalmore goes back to 1839 when the local landowner, Alexander Matheson (also, it's said, an opium trader), built it on the site of an old mill—just like Thomas Mackenzie of Glen Ord—to improve his rent roll and to create industrial jobs to tame his tenants. And like Mackenzie, Matheson immediately rented the business out to a succession of lessees, the last of them being a family called Mackenzie. There are a lot of Mackenzies in these parts! These particular Mackenzies were an enterprising lot who in 1870 exported the first boatload of malt whisky to Australia, who

Dalmore wash backs

doubled the capacity of the distillery, and who eventually, in 1891, bought the freehold of Dalmore.

Many distilleries have a disastrous fire at some point in their lives: Only Dalmore managed to blow itself up. This was during World War I when it was requisitioned to be a munitions factory and—well, someone was careless with a match. It wasn't repaired until 1922, but the Mackenzies stayed at the helm until 1960 when they merged with Whyte & Mackay—which was actually one of Dalmore's biggest customers. Since then Dalmore has been the subject of a lot of discreetly handled investment, but in the stillroom you can still see a copper cooling jacket date-stamped 1874.

Visitor center. Shop. Open Monday through Friday, 10 am to 5 pm, November through March; Monday through Saturday 10 am to 5 pm, April through October. Tours must be booked in advance.

■ *Glenmorangie*

Tain IV19 1PZ. 01862 892477
glenmorangie.com

Not only one of the most widely mispronounced names in whisky—it scans with the fruit—Glenmorangie is also one of the most prestigious as a leading single malt in most markets and a byword for quality round the world.

Glenmorangie was established in 1843 in a former brewery by local distiller William Matheson (no relation, apparently, to the

Glenmorangie is one of the most prestigious leading single malt in most markets and a byword for quality round the world.

Alexander Matheson of Dalmore, above). Displaying admirable thrift, he kitted it out with two second-hand gin-stills from London, where the big gin makers were re-equipping with the newfangled and much more efficient Coffey continuous still; all replacement stills at Glemorangie since then have been based on the same design.

As you will see when you visit, gin stills are much taller than traditional whisky stills and the modern stills at Glenmorangie are, at 16' 10", the tallest in Scotland. The taller the still, the lighter-bodied the spirit; and Glenmorangie also, and unusually, uses hard water drawn from sandstone rather than the peatier burn water. Richer expressions of the whisky derive from the distillery's pioneering use of formerly used port, sherry, and Madeira casks to finish off the maturation.

Glenmorangie was bought from the Mathesons in 1918 by the Leith blenders Macdonald & Muir, who rebuilt and extended it in 1979. In 2004 it was sold, appropriately enough, to the French luxury goods company Louis Vuitton Moet Hennessy, or LVMH for short, and since then has been extended again. The original stillhouse has been converted into a visitor centre and museum whose prize exhibit is an 1880s steam engine: Glenmorangie was the first in Scotland to switch from direct-fired stills to heating by steam coil.

Visitor center. Shop. Museum. Open year-round Monday through Friday, 10 am to 5 pm; also Saturday, 10 am to 4 pm, June through August; and Sunday, 12 noon to 4 pm, July through August. Tours must be pre-booked.

Inverness

One of the delights of a rugged and sparsely populated country like Scotland is its provincial towns and cities. Because they are, in comparison to England, remote from each other, and because they serve enormous rural hinterlands, they generally possess much better facilities than an English city of the same size.

Inverness, dubbed the Capital of the Highlands, is a perfect example. Its population of about 60,000 is actually less than that of many English county towns—Shrewsbury, Stafford, and Lincoln, for example—but it is most definitely in feeling, outlook, institutions and, since 2001, in law, a city. Its combined arts center, **Eden Court**, includes a 1,000-seat auditorium. Its museum and art gallery boasts a world-class collection of 17th and 18th-century silverware. Its university campus has 8,500 undergraduates to liven up the social scene. There's a cathedral, **St. Andrew's**, and a castle now used as law courts (both Victorian). There are tropical gardens at the **Floral Hall** in Bught Lane. There are more than 100 restaurants. And the airport even has its own aviation museum.

For all that, though, most tourists use Inverness as a base for exploring the surrounding Highlands. The battlefield of **Culloden**, where dreams of a Stuart revival were ground into the mud, is two miles away, as is **Loch Ness**: You can try monster-spotting on a luxury cruise. **Cawdor Castle** of Macbeth fame, mountain walks, outdoor activities of all kinds from off-roading to paintballing, the towering **Plodda Falls**, dolphin-spotting in the Moray Firth, the **Beauly** art collection—all of these are within easy reach of the city center. And only a dozen miles or so to the west the wilderness of the Highlands—**Strathconon, Glen Affric, Glen Cannich**—with all its forests, lochs, and 3,000 ft peaks, opens up.

For the whisky tourist, too, Inverness is more of a base than an attraction in its own right. It feels as if it ought to have its own distillery—and until the 1980s it had three. Glen Mhor and Glen Albyn, though, were fatalities in the great Distillers Company purge of 1983, and their bodies were buried under a retail park. Five years later Millburn followed: Its mortal remains now form part of a Premier Inn. Nevertheless with Speyside to the east of it and Black Isle to the north, Inverness has plenty to offer the whisky drinker.

Hotel bars, as in Aberdeen, tend to be unusually and in some cases exceptionally well-stocked with single malts, both in official and independent bottlings. The **Culloden House Hotel** at Culloden regularly has 160 varieties on sale and was a Scottish Malt Whisky Society accredited Embassy; closer to the city center the **Kingsmills Hotel on** Culcabock Rd. is also renowned for its selection. Some restaurants, too, offer a good choice of after-dinner drams: **Nico's Seafood & Grill Room** on Ness Bank has 50. Pubbier pubs with real ale and live music that also specialize in malts include the **Blackfriars** in Academy Street, the **Castle Tavern** in View Place, and the **Hootananny** in Church Street. And for carry-outs, there's a branch of **The Whisky Shop** in Bridge Street.

The countryside around Inverness is also studded with good whisky pubs such as the **Anderson** at Fortrose and the amazing **Fiddlers** at Drumnadrochit, right on the shore of Loch Ness itself. And every year Bogbain, the former farm at Drumossie two miles south of the city on the A9, which has converted all its historic barns and outbuildings into characterful and idiosyncratic venues, hosts a one-day whisky festival supported by many leading distilleries.

■ *Glen Ord*

Muir of Ord IV6 7UJ. 01463 872004
discovering-distilleries.com

We owe Glen Ord to the enlightenment of an "improving" landlord, Thomas Mackenzie, descendant of an ancient aristocratic family, who inherited the local estate in 1820 and set about the twin tasks of improving both its value and the moral condition of the tenantry. Part of this great work was the building in 1837 of the Glen Ord distillery to create disciplined employment for his tenants, drive the bothie distillers out of business, and generate a rent for himself. It also, by the by, competed with the eight other legal stills in the Black Isle, which one by one went out of business.

Mackenzie didn't run the distillery himself, of course—it was leased to two local businessmen who, 10 years later, went bust. New tenants followed; the distillery was expanded in 1877, burned down in 1878 (this happened a lot with distilleries, for obvious reasons), was rebuilt, and finally in 1896 was sold to a Dundee blender, James Watson & Co. Watson's sold up to Dewar's in 1923; Dewar's sold up to the Distillers Company in 1925; the Distillers Company eventually morphed into Diageo. And through it all, Glen Ord soldiered on efficiently and successfully, gradually being expanded and extended, with the huge new maltings being added in 1968 to supply a number of DCL distilleries.

Glen Ord; photo courtesy of Diageo

It was expanded yet again in 2013 as demand in the Asian markets—where The Singleton of Ord is a popular malt—continued to grow.

In the 1990s a visitor center and shop were added, along with an exhibition of local history and heritage. It's not the prettiest of places, Glen Ord; but if you like your appreciation of good malt whisky spiced up by the addition of the period drama of Scottish landed families and their tenants and business associates, this is the place for you!

Visitor center. Shop. Exhibition. Standard tours and Tasting Experience tours—check website for opening times.

■ Loch Ewe

Drumchork Estate, Aultbea IV22 2HU. 01445 731242
lochewedistillery.co.uk

Aultbea on Loch Ewe way over on the west coast near Ullapool may not be the remotest place in Scotland, but after the twisting 70-mile drive along the A835 and A832 from Inverness it can feel like it. However it was a destination already known to diehard whisky-lovers even before Drumchork Lodge hoteliers John Clotworthy and Frances Oates installed a miniature distillery in a derelict garage there in 2004, because the Lodge was already world-famous for its selection of 700+ single malts.

The partners had to go to the very edge of legality to recreate a pre-1823 Excise Act bothie distillery. Their 120-L stills were less than a tenth of the minimum size of 1,800 L then allowed by customs, and it was only their discovery of a legal loophole (now closed!) permitting private licenses for small stills that persuaded the authorities to let Loch Ewe start up in the first place. The pursuit of absolute authenticity was nearly stopped again at the water's edge: The Scottish Environmental Protection Agency wouldn't let them use untreated burn water, so the mashing liquor comes from the hotel's tap and has to be treated to remove the chlorine.

But they are absolutely authentic in that they make not a drop of whisky: The law says that whisky must be three years old, and since John and Frances believe (and not without reason) that the illegal distillers of old didn't go in for long maturation but drank their moonshine fresh, they're not ageing theirs either. What you will drink straight from the open cask in the bar at the Lodge is therefore officially "spirit."

All this is for your benefit: The entire operation was aimed at bringing visitors in to experience the moonshiner's world of two centuries ago. You can tour the tiny distillery—it will take you all of 15 minutes—or you can stay for five days learning the art of whisky-making for yourself and visiting the sea-caves where the moonshiners once practiced their art. And at the end of it, you get to take home your own five-liter cask of... "spirit." However by the time you read this it probably won't be Frances and John you meet at Loch Ewe: They've decided to retire and have put the whole enterprise on the market. Let's just hope that whoever buys it runs it the way they've always done.

Check website for details of visits, accommodation, and five-day Whisky Experience.

Tomatin open mash tun for visitor viewing; photo ©Ewen Weatherspoon

■ *Tomatin*

Tomatin IV13 7YT. 01463 248144
tomatin.com

High in the hills and miles from anywhere stands what was once Scotland's biggest malt whisky distillery. To the modern eye the siting of some of these distilleries is a mystery, because these days we look first at the ease of distributing the finished product. To the founders of the Tomatin Spey Distillery Co. back in 1897, ease of access to raw materials was a much more pressing logistical problem: After all, if there's no railhead at hand you can still get barrels of finished whisky down to the nearest goods yard by cart; but try transporting all the water, peat, and barley you need for any distance... well, mystery solved. Hence the existence of Tomatin, 1,500 ft up on the A9 halfway between Inverness and Aviemore—so remote that the workforce still lives in tied cottages surrounding the distillery.

Tomatin got along soundly and unspectacularly supplying high-quality fillings to blenders for 60 years, but in the 1950s, with the post-war recovery gathering pace, started expanding. Over the next 30 years capacity was added in successive waves until at its height it was operating 27 stills with a potential output of 12 million liters. Then in the late 1970s three nightmares caught up with Tomatin all at once: Many of the stills were beginning to wear out; there was a huge downturn in world demand for scotch; and as it had always rubbed along just supplying fillings it had never developed a brand of its own. In 1984 it went bust.

Eyebrows were raised in 1986 when two investors, a distilling company and a hotel chain, bought and reopened Tomatin. They were Japanese—how serious could they be? Well, very! They rationalized production, reducing the number of stills to 12; they marketed blends including Legacy, The Antiquary range, The Talisman, and Big T around the world; they released single malts at various ages. Tomatin had slimmed down... but less, in this case, was definitely more.

They also opened a visitor center rated four stars by the Scottish Tourist Board, with attractions including one of the industry's few remaining working cooperages. There is a standard tour with DVD and complimentary dram and a longer (and more expensive!) presentation and tasting tour.

Visitor center. Shop. Open Monday through Friday, 10 am to 5 pm, November through April; Monday through Saturday 10 am to 5 pm, Sunday 12:30 pm to 4:30 pm, May through October (no tours on Sundays). Tours must be booked in advance.

Elgin

If Speyside has a capital, the former county town of Morayshire is surely it. Elgin may be Scotland's smallest city, with a population of less than 30,000; but its former eminence is revealed by its best-known landmark, **Elgin Cathedral**—a ruined 14th-century cathedral, once the grandest Gothic church in the land.

It's hard to think of Elgin as an industrial city now, but with the arrival of the railway in 1852—at first only linking Elgin to Lossiemouth five miles away, but then extended inland up the Spey valley—that's what it became. Distilling and its allied trades were, of course, of paramount importance; but other industries flourished as well. **Johnstons of Elgin** cashmere mill dates from 1797 and is the last of its kind in Scotland; its shop, mill tours, and coffee shop make it one of the city's leading attractions. The **Moray Motor Museum** in Bridge Street, with its collection of over 40 classic cars and motorbikes in racing condition, makes another interesting diversion from the subject of whisky.

But what does Elgin offer the whisky tourist? Of the seven distilleries in and around the city only Glen Moray is open to the public; but it's within easy walking distance of the center (as is everywhere in Elgin!), on the southwestern edge of town not far from Dr. Gray's Hospital. There's a plethora of hotel bars and lounge bars with a tally of malts to make a strong man despair—the **Laichmoray**, Maisondieu Street (130); the **Sunninghill**, Hay Street, (100+); the Drouthy Cobbler, High Street (130). But Elgin is also home to one of the great temples of malt—not a distillery, nor a bar, but a shop. **Gordon & MacPhail** on South Street is Scotland's oldest independent (or "merchant") bottler, founded as a grocer and wine merchant in 1895. For more than a century it has specialized in bottling single malts that were usually only found in blends, often at full cask strength (anything from 57% ABV upwards), often at extreme ages. Many distillers didn't take to this and, even though they didn't bottle their own malts, didn't care for anyone else doing it either and tried to stop them. But to connoisseurs all over the world Gordon

& MacPhail (along with Cadenhead's of Campbeltown) was their only source of rare bottlings, and the business thrived. Gordon & MacPhail even owns its own distillery now, Benromach. Impossible to be in Elgin and not to visit!

Benriach Distillery; photo ©Peter Sanground

■ *Benriach*
Longmorn, Elgin IV30 8SJ. 01343 862888
benriachdistillery.co.uk

Ancient or modern? Benriach may have been built in 1898, but it closed after just two years following the collapse of its biggest customer. It wasn't fully reopened until 1965, so you will have to make your own mind up whether it's about to celebrate its 120th birthday, or has just celebrated its 50th.

It was originally built during the great whisky boom by John Duff, right next door to his Longmorn distillery on the A941 just a couple of miles south of the town. Only its traditional floor malting, complete with obligatory Charles Doig pagoda, survived the closure, continuing to supply Longmorn for 101 years while the distillery buildings themselves moldered slowly away. In 1965, however, the shell of the distillery was re-equipped and reopened by its then parent company, Glenlivet; and its capacity was actually doubled in 1985; but in 2002, after a string of takeovers, it was declared surplus to new owner Pernod Ricard's requirements and fell silent once more.

Like a number of unwanted distilleries, though, it was quickly revived by a well-capitalized enthusiast—in this case master blender and industry executive Billy Walker. Since then the floor maltings, which had been closed for 13 years, has been thoroughly refurbished and reopened, a bewildering array of different expressions has been released, and Mr. Walker and his partners have also bought Glendronach in the Eastern Highlands and Glenglassaugh on the Moray coast.

Connoisseurs' Tour Tuesday and Thursday, 10 am and 2pm. Minimum party of 4. Booking essential.

■ *Benromach*
Invererne Rd., Forres IV36 3EB. 01309 675968
benromach.com

A distillery with a distinctly checkered history, Benromach is one of an increasing number that have found their niche under independent and enthusiastic ownership.

It was built in 1898–1899 by the great architect of the industry Charles Doig, but the slump that followed the collapse of one of the country's biggest blenders meant it didn't open until 1909—only to close again when World War I broke out. In 1925 it fell silent yet

Benromach; photo © John Paul Photography

again owing to the combined effects of Prohibition and the Great Depression, but was bought and reopened by an American-owned company in 1937… just in time for World War II!

After the war it was bought by The Distillers Company and ticked along for 30 years, until in 1983 it was named as one of the nine selected for closure as the economy worsened. And so it remained for 10 years when it was bought by the independent Elgin bottler, Gordon & MacPhail. By now it had to be completely re-equipped, and the new plant installed by Gordon & MacPhail makes Benromach Speyside's smallest distillery. And one of its most visitable, too: The award-winning Malt Whisky Centre, complete with shop and museum, was declared open by Prince Charles in October 1998, was refurbished in 2009, and has even more recently been extended to include more tasting rooms. Tours and displays feature not only the distillery's own history but also that of its owner, which is one of a handful of independent or merchant bottlers that over the years have done so much to keep the traditions and mysteries of malt whisky alive.

Visitor center. Shop. Four levels of tour from standard to Distillery Manager's conducted tour. For opening times please check website.

■ Glen Moray

Bruceland Rd., Elgin IV30 1YE. 01343 550900
glenmoray.com

As Speyside's principal town, Elgin might almost be called the Capital of Whisky, but it only has one distillery actually within its bounds—Glen Moray. And not unnaturally, with Elgin full of tourists, Glen Moray is very welcoming to visitors.

An attractive group of stone buildings clustered round a sunny courtyard (Elgin and its surroundings have more sunny days, on average, than any other part of Scotland), from some vantage points Glen Moray could almost be a Cotswold farm. It started life as Arnot's Brewery but was converted in 1897 to take advantage of the whisky boom that was going on. The boom didn't last, and Glen Moray fell silent in 1910; but in 1927 it was bought by the owners of the much more famous Glenmorangie and Ardbeg distilleries. It was always something of the poor relation in such a prestigious family, though, and in 2008 it was sold off to a French multinational,

Glen Moray; photo © John Paul Photography

La Martiniquaise, whose roots—as you might guess from the name—lie in the rum trade.

Since it came out from under Glenmorangie's shadow, though, Glen Moray has become more assertive: It has had a visitor center since 2004 but now it has a deluxe tour, The Fifth Chapter, as well as the standard; and if you're feeling flush you can even bottle your own straight from the cask.

Visitor center. Shop. Cafe. Open year-round Monday through Friday, 9 am to 5 pm (five tours), plus 10 am to 4:30 pm Saturday (four tours), May through September. Booking essential for Fifth Chapter tour.

Rothes

For a village of no more than 1,200 souls Rothes does a remarkably good job of hiding its five distilleries—even the plume of white steam you might see as you approach comes not from a distillery but from a plant that turns spent grain and pot ale into animal feed. However the distilleries in and around Rothes that do welcome tourists are three of the biggest names in the whisky world.

Rothes has medieval origins, but all that remains of them is a short stretch of stone wall on a low hill that was once Rothes Castle. The existing village was planned and laid out by the local landowner in 1766: Its main delight to the whisky tourist—apart from the distilleries themselves, of course is its quartet of outstanding and completely different whisky bars.

The **Eastbank Hotel's** selection of 105 malts would be respectable in most towns. In Rothes, though, the **Quaich Bar** at the magnificent late Victorian **Craigellachie Hotel** has 700 malts on sale, the dearest of them costing £275 per measure. **The Highlander** aims for a more homely, more "village inn" ambience—but few village inns commission their own bottlings of rare single malts or offer whisky breakfasts. Finally there's the tiny **Fiddichside Inn**, which was run by Dorothy Brandie until her death aged 89 in 2009. She had lived in the pub since infancy. It too has a more than respectable selection of malts.

Cardhu; photo courtesy of Diageo

■ *Cardhu*
Knockando AB38 7RY. 01479 874635
discovering-distilleries.com

They were good neighbors, John and Helen Cummings. Leasing Cardhu Farm in 1811, they promptly started making whisky illegally—Helen, according to legend, being the actual distiller—and when the gauger came they would sit him down to lunch while Helen went out with a big red flag to warn all the other moonshiners in the surrounding hills. After the 1823 Excise Act they went legit, although for many decades distilling was a sideline to farming. When John died in 1842 the farm and distillery went to their son and daughter-in-law, Lewis and Elizabeth; but it wasn't until 1885 that Elizabeth, by then long widowed and an energetic and capable businesswoman, rebuilt the distillery on a much bigger scale on an adjoining site. At the same time she gave William Grant (of Glenfiddich fame) his start in the industry by selling him the old stills for a knockdown £120.

In 1893, very shortly before Elizabeth's death, Cardhu was sold for a whopping £20,000 to John Walker & Sons of Kilmarnock, to become the dominant malt in the Johnnie Walker blend. Walker's eventually became part of the Distillers Company, with Johnnie Walker itself one of its global best-sellers. In the 1960s the old distillery was hugely expanded to permit a dramatic increase in production, while Cardhu was launched as a single malt in the now-familiar corked decanter format in which it is now one of the world top 10 malts.

Despite the many new buildings, Cardhu's setting on rising ground overlooking the village of Knockando just off the B9102, its long views towards the hills, and the retention of many charming stone warehouses and maltings make it a beautiful place to visit. It's had a visitor center since 1988 and runs three grades of tour: Standard, classic, and the Cardhu Collection.

Visitor center. Shop. Check website for opening times. Book Classic and Cardhu Collection tours in advance.

■ Glen Grant

Elgin Rd., Rothes AB38 7BS. 01340 832118
glengrant.com

Meet the first of three dynasties of Grants. The brothers James & John founded Glen Grant in 1840 having previously leased the original Aberlour and (reputedly) distilled illegally on the family farm.

The brothers were very forward-looking: They were influential in the building of the local railway line in 1851, and Glen Grant had the first electric lighting in the Highlands when a generator was installed in 1861. The next in the dynasty—James's son, also called James but always known as "The Major"—was the first man in the district to own a car. He also, on a hunting trip to Matabeleland in 1898, adopted an orphan named Biawa, who became his butler and lived at the family home until his death in 1972.

In 1897 The Major decided to expand the distillery by building a sister plant, Glen Grant 2, across the road: The two were connected by a pipeline over the street. However GG2 fell victim to the crash of 1900 and closed two years later. It was reopened in 1965 under a new name, Caperdonich, but closed again in 2002, this time seemingly for good.

Glen Grant achieved huge success in the export markets and in 1953 merged with another and perhaps even more famous Speyside

As one of the most handsome and elegant of Scottish distilleries, with its baronial-style pepperpot turrets and crowstep gables, Glen Grant was crying out to be opened to the public long before 2008, when a brand-new visitor center was finally built in the old coach house.... The fabulous 22-acre gardens are also open to the public.

name, G&J Smith's Glenlivet, acquiring Longmorn a little later. In 1978 the combine was bought by Seagram of Canada: The last of the dynasty was The Major's grandson, Douglas MacKessack. Via various corporate shenanigans the distillery was bought by Campari in 2006, Glen Grant being Italy's (and one of the world's) best-selling single malt.

As one of the most handsome and elegant of Scottish distilleries, with its baronial-style pepperpot turrets and crowstep gables, Glen Grant was crying out to be opened to the public long before 2008, when a brand-new visitor center was finally built in the old coach house featuring a recreation of The Major's study. The fabulous 22-acre gardens are also open to the public.

Visitor center. Shop. Open year-round Monday through Saturday, 9:30 am to 5 pm; Sunday 12 noon to 5 pm; last tour 4 pm.

■ ◆*Macallan*

Easter Elchies, Craigellachie AB38 9RX. 01340 872280
themacallan.com

The new-look Macallan distillery will amaze and delight you. For although it was one of the first distilleries in the region established after the 1823 Excise Act, what you actually see when you arrive… well, if they make whisky in the Shire, they make it in a distillery that looks something like this one.

The Macallan was something of a plodder for the first 140-odd years of its life. It changed hands a few times in its early years, then achieved a respectable stability in the early 20th century as a family trust that just went on. In the 1960s, though, it became a public company whose new management immediately set about galvanizing the distillery, doubling its size and taking two pioneering decisions: First, to revive the old custom of finishing the whisky in old sherry casks; and second, actively promoting it as a single malt rather than just a blender's favorite.

The new, richer, flavor—although criticized by some—was a huge hit and Macallan quickly acquired its reputation as one of the true aristocrats of the malt whisky world. Equally quickly, its world-beating potential attracted investors including Japanese distiller Suntory, which bought a 25% stake in 1986. Ten years later it was bought by Highland Distillers and thus soon became—along

Macallan

with Highland Park—the jewel in the crown of Highland's purchaser, the Edrington Group.

Despite all this glory, and despite its stunning position in the Elchies Forest just west of Craigellachie with stunning views over the Spey to Ben Rinnes, the distillery was slow to throw its doors open to the public. To be honest, the old distillery wasn't actually all that attractive, and a visitor center didn't come until 2001. When it did, though, it was a big success.

If you've ever visited in the past, though, you wouldn't recognize the place now. Ground was broken in December 2014 on a totally new £100 million plant that's revolutionary in both design and construction. The successive stages of production are laid out in a linear series of cells, each with its own conical timber-framed roof. This row of roofs is entirely clad with turf to create the illusion of a range of hills; but it's not just for show. The turf is also a near-perfect insulator, and to cap it all the heating and electricity are all supplied by a

£74 million biomass generator on a 12-acre site next door that also supplies low-carbon electricity to 20,000 Speyside homes.

The new plant will produce 15 million liters a year, compared to the 9.5 million liters the old plant (which is being mothballed) could turn out. And the development, which is due to open in spring 2017, also includes a completely new immersive visitor exhibition, a gallery, and a cafe.

Visitor center. Shop. Check website for new opening times and tours.

Dufftown

If Elgin can claim to be the capital of Speyside, Dufftown has an equally good claim to be the capital of malt. "Rome was built on seven hills, Dufftown stands on seven stills," goes the rhyme, and at times in the town's history it has even been true. Sometimes there have been as many as nine; at present there are five (or six, if you count Kininvie as a separate entity from Balvenie). Nevertheless, for a town of no more than 2,000 souls Dufftown does produce a prodigious amount of malt: The eponymous distillery itself is one of the biggest in Scotland; and Glenfiddich turns out a pretty heroic quantity of the stuff. Dufftown reckons to contribute more per head to Scotland's balance of payments than any other town or city in the country.

Like so many others in the Highlands, this was a planned town, the improving landlord in this case being James Duff, Earl of Fife, and the date of foundation being 1817. The impressive remains of **Balvenie Castle** (Historic Scotland: Open seven days 9:30 am to 5:30 pm, April through September) with its massive curtain walls show that the site was settled—and important—long before then; but the grid-pattern of streets lined with neat Georgian facades is absolutely typical of planned towns of the period and of the orderly mindset of the lairds who built them.

Even if whisky hadn't brought you here you'd find plenty to see and do in and around the town. The **Loch Park Outdoor Adventure Centre** with its canoeing, raft-building, gorge-walking, fishing, archery and other healthy pursuits is only three miles away on the B9104 Keith Rd.; there is a renowned golf club; the countryside offers hill-walking including one **Corbett**, Ben Rinnes at 2,775 ft, as well as level routes especially popular with cyclists. For steam buffs, the 11-mile **Dufftown-Keith Railway** was reopened by volunteers in 2001 and has a collection of vintage locos and rolling stock to enjoy. And the **Highland Games** held on the last Saturday of every July are also well known for the number of pipe bands that perform.

For the whisky tourist, Dufftown has more to offer than just distillery tours. On Fife Street there's the small **Dufftown Whisky Museum** as well as a branch of **The Whisky Shop,** the **Royal Oak Inn** with a range of 125 malts, and the **Tannochbrae Guest House** and restaurant, whose **Stables Bar** has an astonishing selection of 300 malts. (There are even more to choose from—a mind-numbing 700, to be precise—at the **Grouse at Cabrach** eight miles south of Dufftown on the A941). The **Taste of Speyside Restaurant** in Balvenie Street also has a more than respectable range of 80 malts to browse.

Dufftown is also the epicentre of Speyside's four-day **Autumn Whisky Festival,** held every year since 2006 at the end of that other "shoulder month," September. It's not on quite the same scale as the **Spirit of Speyside** event in April; but with 90 events in such a small town it's much more compact and perhaps easier to navigate. The walking tour of all Dufftown's distilleries is a particularly popular highlight.

■ *Balvenie/Kininvie*
Dufftown AB55 4BB. 01340 820373
thebalvenie.com

So close to Glenfiddich that they're almost a single site, Balvenie for many years played second fiddle to its slightly older sister. The founder of both distilleries, William Grant, was a canny man: He saved money by equipping Glenfiddich with second-hand stills, and when in 1893 he decided to build Balvenie (to cash in on a disastrous fire at Glenlivet that led to a serious run on stocks for blending), he not only found yet more cheap second-hand stills, he also found a cheap second-hand building. Balvenie New House had been designed by the Adam brothers themselves in 1724 but had long been derelict: The distillery malting was fitted into part of it, while dressed stone from more ruinous parts was recycled to build the distillery itself.

During the last half-century while Glenfiddich was being established as Britain's most popular single malt, Balvenie was always regarded as more of a connoisseur's dram—indeed one noted critic has described its 15-year-old expression as the best whisky in Scotland. And although Glenfiddich itself is now available in a multitude of expressions (one bottling was over a century old), Balvenie has

Balvenie

always seemed the more exclusive and more traditional of the two. It grows its own barley, and malts it, too, in one of Scotland's few surviving old-fashioned floor maltings; it has its own coppersmiths and coopers; and its tours are serious matters for connoisseurs only.

The Balvenie site is also home to a new stillhouse, built in 1990 and christened Kininvie, whose washbacks are housed in an extension to the Balvenie building. Kininvie produces whisky for blending only.

Connoisseur Tours must be booked in advance; maximum of 8 per tour.

■ *Glenfiddich*
Dufftown AB55 4DH. 01340 820373
glenfiddich.com

Here at the home of the world's best-known malt whisky they will regale you with the biography of its founder, the truly remarkable William Grant. Born in 1839, the son of an ex-soldier, he worked his way up from farm boy to apprentice cobbler to distillery book-keeper, learning and saving as he went, until at the age of nearly 50 he seized the chance to buy a couple of clapped-out old pot stills at a bargain price, lease a bit of land and build a distillery of his own (and pretty much on his own, too, although all his seven sons were dragooned into laboring for him). It was such a success

Glenfiddich

that four years later he built a second, Balvenie, just next door. And when, four years after that, his and indeed the industry's biggest customer, Pattison's, went bust, instead of following dozens of others into bankruptcy he launched a blend of his own—Grant's Standfast, still hugely popular today.

William Grant died aged 89 in 1923, but the company is still owned and run by his direct descendants, and they have never stopped innovating. In 1963 Glenfiddich became the first single malt to be aggressively promoted in the global market; others have followed, but only a handful have had anything like Glenfiddich's success. And in 1969 the distillery became the first to open its doors to the world when it created a visitor center—recently refurbished at a cost of nearly £2 million. Yet the innovation has not come at the expense of tradition: There are still coppersmiths and coopers on site, and some of the malt at least comes from the old floor-maltings at Balvenie.

Visitor center. Shop. Restaurant. Bar. Standard tours hourly 9:30 am to 4:30 pm. Book ahead for Explorers and Pioneers tours.

 Aberlour

Aberlour is a planned town which was laid out by Charles Grant of Elchies in 1812; hence its full name, Charlestown of Aberlour. Nothing could be more Scottish than its high street, which has the Aberlour distillery at one end and Scotland's biggest shortbread bakery, **Walkers**, at the other. A landmark in Aberlour is the **clock tower**—not a municipal one, but all that's left of the celebrated Aberlour Orphanage. This was founded by the Rev. Charles Jupp in 1882 and at its peak housed 500 orphans. The orphanage itself was closed in 1967 and subsequently demolished, but its work goes on—the Aberlour Childcare Trust is today one of Scotland's biggest children's charities.

The whisky-lover, having toured the distillery, will stop for refreshment at the **Mash Tun**, a late Victorian pub in Broomfield Square on the banks of the Spey whose whisky bar stocks—among many other joys—exclusive Glenfarclas Family Casks stretching back 46 years. "Founder's Reserve" and "Family Reserve" are premium tags you will find used and, more often, misused on high-end brands of all sorts of products: These Family Casks are the real McCoy!

Ten miles further down on the same side is Ballindalloch, a tiny village built round a bridge over one of the Spey's tributaries, the Avon, and home to Glenfarclas and Cragganmore. Ballindalloch is famous for its castle, **Ballindalloch Castle**, an incredibly romantic and beautiful Scottish baronial pile justly nicknamed the Pearl of the North. The oldest part—the massive central tower with its crow-stepped gables and pepper-pot cupola, was built in 1546 by the McPherson-Grant family which still lives there. The more elegant wings were added in the 17th and 18th centuries. It is perhaps best-known for its grounds with 17th-century dovecote, magnificent walled garden, 1937 rock garden, and fishing in the Spey and Avon; but the castle itself is open in summer (10:30 am to 5:30 pm, Monday through Friday, April through September) and contains an important collection of 17th-century Spanish paintings.

At this point, you may want to get your walking boots on. You can't, after all, come to the Highlands without putting in at least one good hike; and if you haven't the week or so necessary to navigate the entire 66-mile Speyside way you might as well do its 15-mile Ballindalloch-Tomintoul spur, which passes the door of The Glenlivet itself. But don't think you're getting off lightly: The spur includes some of the most strenuous terrain the "**Speyway**" has to offer including two 1,800 ft summits and lots of soggy, boggy moorlands that demand decent waterproof boots. The weather is also unbelievably changeable, so even on the (apparently) sunniest day take a sweater and waterproofs in your rucksack.

Most people do the spur uphill from Ballindalloch, but to get the most out of the charming village of Tomintoul—at 1,160 ft it's the highest in Scotland—it might be a good idea to start at the top. Tomintoul may be tiny, with a resident population of only 300; but it has a deli, a craft studio, a post office, two hotels (a third is closed at time of writing, but might reopen), a highly regarded restaurant, a youth hostel, innumerable B&Bs, a museum with reconstructions of a crofter's kitchen and a blacksmith's forge, and the superlative **Whisky Castle.**

Not many villages this size can boast a specialist shop with something like 600 single malts on its shelves; but there's more than even that to the Whisky Castle. It specializes in unfiltered whiskies, none of which are color-balanced with caramel. That means that almost all of its malts are special bottlings rather than the official bottlings that come liquored down to 40% ABV, chill-filtered to get rid of the resulting haze, and color-equalized. A treasure trove indeed!

Tomintoul, if you decide to stop here awhile, is also a fantastic outdoor pursuits center on the very edge of the **Cairngorms National Park** with canoeing, gorge walking, Nordic and downhill skiing all close at hand. And, of course, walking. The Spur isn't a circular walk: You'll have to leave your car (only way to get here, alas) at Tomintoul and arrange in advance with your hotel or B&B to be picked up at Ballindalloch and ferried home in the evening. The whole walk is waymarked with a thistle symbol and should take you about 6–7 hours, so have a good breakfast and take a packed lunch. There are two fairly arduous ascents, so you need to be in reasonable condition (the views from the tops make the effort well worth it); The Glenlivet distillery with its visitor center and cafe is midway between them if you need a reviving cuppa, although you'll want to make a separate trip for the distillery tour. Once you reach Ballindaloch, the **Delnashaugh Hotel** might be a convenient place to await your lift back up the mountains.

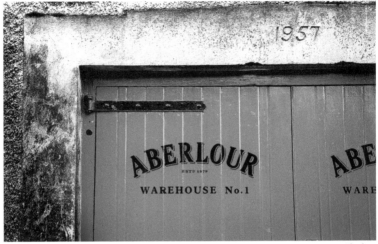

Aberlour

■ *Aberlour*

Aberlour AB38 9PJ. 01340 881249
maltwhiskydistilleries.com

Water is a serious matter around here, and has been for centuries. In the grounds of the distillery at the western end of Aberlour's high street is St. Drostan's Well, supposedly used by the 7th-century missionary to baptize local heathens—and probably sacred, therefore, long before he arrived. And before the distilling industry moved out if the shadows the Spey and its tributaries were lined with watermills, grinding the barley for which this district was renowned. The water that concerns us, though, is the rainwater that filters through the granite slopes of the looming Ben Rinnes range, filling the springs of Aberlour and pure enough to be used untreated.

The distillery was built in 1870 by a grain merchant, James Russell, and succeeded a much earlier venture of the same name that was burning down even while Russell's was abuilding. A noted philanthropist, Russell also funded Aberlour's town hall and cottage hospital. The distillery you see is not his work, though: His was (also!) burnt down in 1898 and was rebuilt by the great architect of distilleries, Charles Doig. It is also noteworthy as the first of many malt distilleries to be bought by Pernod-Ricard, back in 1974 when the French pastis giant was just beginning to venture out into the world.

It's not just the water that's taken seriously here: It's the visitor experience as well. The visitor center built in 2002 was always intended more for the connoisseur than the general tourist: Standard tours take nearly two hours rather than the standard one, and include not just a free dram but a tutored tasting; the deluxe Founder's Experience takes three hours.

Visitor center open seven days 9:30 am to 5 pm, March through October; Monday through Friday, 9:30 am to 4 pm, October through December. All tours must be booked in advance.

■ Ballindalloch

Lagmore AB37 9AA. 01807 500331
ballindallochdistillery.com

The pretty-well perfect Scottish baronial Ballindalloch Castle with its surrounding estate has long been one of the few attractions on Speyside that had little or nothing to do with whisky. The 16th-century castle itself, with its turrets and crenellations; the beautiful grounds; the golf; the wildlife; the country sports—this is the Scotland you'd dreamed about. And to make it even more charming, Guy McPherson-Grant is the 23rd generation of his family to own it.

But still, this is Speyside, where everything revolves around whisky; and in 2011 Mr. McPherson-Smith hatched a plan to convert a derelict 200-year-old farmstead on the estate into, guess what, a distillery. The restoration was carefully carried out by tradesmen either from the estate itself or nearby, using local materials where possible. The plan, echoing the 1820s when the estate last had its own distillery at Delnashaugh (now a hotel) just across the golf course, was to distil with Ballindalloch's own barley, using the pot ale to condition the soil on which it grew and the spent grains to feed the estate's Aberdeen Angus beef herd. Even master distiller Charlie

Unlike many new distilleries Ballindalloch isn't trifling with gin, or vodka, or immature spirit: The intention is to give the maturing stocks at least eight years in oak before seeing how it's turned out.

Smith, who supervised the installation of the copperwork and now presides over its operation, is hardly a stranger, having spent part of his career at Cardhu just across the Spey. Ballindalloch may be exaggerating when it calls itself Scotland's only single-estate whisky, but it can't be faulted for trying.

The first new make ran from the stills in September 2014 and in April 2015 the Duke and Duchess of Rothesay (or, as they're known elsewhere, Prince Charles and Lady Camilla) popped in to cut the ribbon. Unlike many new distilleries Ballindalloch isn't trifling with gin, or vodka, or immature spirit: The intention is to give the maturing stocks at least eight years in oak before seeing how it's turned out.

Tours by appointment, Monday through Friday. Basic tour £35, 2–3 hours, parties of eight. Ballindalloch Spirit £75, parties of eight. Art of Whisky Making £175, 8 am to 4 pm, parties of two. Designated drivers free.

■ Cragganmore
Ballindalloch AB37 9AB. 01479 874700
discovering-distilleries.com

Often credited to Charles Doig—although if he had been involved he would have been 14 and still at school—Cragganmore was built in 1869 on a farm leased from the local estate by John Smith, former distillery manager at Macallan, Glenfarclas, and Glenlivet, and reputedly the illegitimate son of Glenlivet founder George Smith. A forward-looking man, Smith chose the location to take advantage of the railway (now the Speyside Way, courtesy of Dr. Beeching), and soon after his in 1886 regular Whisky Special freight trains laden with casks of Cragganmore were leaving Ballindalloch station.

His son John Jr. inherited the distillery and commissioned Doig (really, this time) to expand it in 1901; he died in 1912, leaving it to his widow Mary Jane who ran it herself for 11 years before selling it to the Distillers Company.

A smallish distillery whose product was always rated A1 by blenders, its single bottlings were never widely available, and DCL's successor Diageo surprised everyone except a handful of more knowledgeable aficionados by selecting it as Speyside's representative in its Classic Malt range in 1998. The quality of its output

Cragganmore; photo © Angus Bremner

combined with its tranquil location in a secluded glen overlooking the Spey off the A95 near Bridge of Avon make for a peaceful and informative visit, especially as it's not so well known and heavily frequented as some other Speyside distilleries. An upgrade to the Expressions tour earns you a tasting in the sumptuous Cragganmore Clubroom.

Shop. Open Monday through Friday, April through October 9:30 am to 5 pm. Last standard tour 4 pm; last Expressions tour 3pm.

■ Glenfarclas
Ballindalloch AB37 9BD. 01807 500345
glenfarclas.co.uk

Scotland only has two or three whisky companies that could be called "family firms" in the sense that the direct descendants of the founders still own or at least control them. One is William Grant of Glenfiddich fame. John Grant—no relation—is another.

The Glenfarclas distillery in Ballindalloch on the A95 five miles south of Aberlour was already 30 years old when John Grant bought it in 1865. He himself was twice as old as the distillery, and his real interest was in the farm on which Glenfarclas was sited. For the first five years he leased the whisky business to one John Smith; but when Smith went off to found a distillery of his own at Cragganmore, Grant and his son George decided to run Glenfarclas

The new Glenfarclas was noted for possessing the biggest stills on Speyside. Today these stills remain direct-fired, a method of heating that creates caramel.

themselves. John died in 1889, his son just a year later. And so a third generation—another George—found himself in charge at the tender age of 16. Nevertheless, he grew into the job, and in 1897 commissioned the building of an entirely new distillery on the site. The new Glenfarclas was noted for possessing the biggest stills on Speyside. Today these stills remain direct-fired, a method of heating that creates caramel. This, together with the sherry casks in which Glenfarclas is matured, gives it the full-bodied richness for which it is still famous.

Since George II we've had George III, John II, and now George IV. But being family doesn't mean the Grants are stuffy: They opened a visitor center way back in 1973, decorating it with paneling taken from an ocean liner, the *Empress of Australia*; they were also pioneers in developing a huge range of "expressions"—bottling of various ages, strengths, and finishes—which, these days, everybody seems to do.

Visitor center. Shop. Open Monday through Friday 10 am to 4 pm, October through March; Monday through Friday 10 am to 5 pm, April through June; Monday through Friday 10 am to 5 pm, Saturday 10 am to 4 pm, July through September. Last tour 90 minutes before closing. Connoisseurs Tasting & Tour 2 pm Fridays, July through September, must be booked in advance.

■ *The Glenlivet*

Minmore, Ballindalloch AB37 9DB. 01340 821720
theglenlivet.com

One of Scotch whisky's biggest names, The Glenlivet was founded in 1823 by one of Scotch whisky's biggest characters. The valley of the Livet, 14 miles long and 6 miles wide, was home to a reputed 200 illegal distillers before the Excise Act, and was traded far and wide almost openly. The Smith family of Upper Drumin Farm, high on the barley-growing plateau, was no better than its neighbors and seems to have been moonshining since the 1770s; but sensing the opportunity presented by the 1823 Excise Act, George Smith became the first distiller in Scotland to take out a licensed.

It did not endear him to his neighbors, who saw that their business was being taken away; but, permanently armed with a pair of pistols presented to him by the Laird of Aberlour (he only ever

The Glenlivet

fired them in anger once, and that was to scare a braggart), George prospered. In the 1840s he leased a second distillery to cope with demand; but even two were not enough, and a new, much bigger plant was planned on a new site near the farm. Then in 1858 Upper Drumin was burnt down, so the new distillery, on today's site at Minmore, was completed in a rush.

George Smith died in 1871 and was succeeded by his son John Gordon Smith, whose first job was to face down the legion of imitators seeking to cash in on Glenlivet's success by appropriating its name. By threatening legal action, based on the fact that Minmore was the only distillery in the parish of Glenlivet, he won a victory of sorts. Only whisky from Minmore could be called "The" Glenlivet: Competitors could only use the name as a prefix or suffix. At one time more than 30 did, some of them 30 miles away; the practice, though, has died out, and the only Glenlivet on sale today is The Glenlivet.

Glenlivet remained family-controlled until 1953, when it merged with J&J Grant of Glen Grant fame; 20 years later it merged again, with Longmorn. Then in 1977, at a time of depression in the world market, it was sold to Seagram and thus found its way into the hands of its current owner, Pernod-Ricard subsidiary Chivas Brothers. Only recently the distillery has been doubled in size; and despite its dramatic setting on its windswept plateau, it isn't what you'd call picturesque. That's no excuse for not visiting the world's most famous whisky distillery, though. It's not even all that remote, being only a few miles along the B9008 from Ballindalloch, and is well-signposted. There's a visitor center in the old maltings, and as well as the standard tour there's an in-depth Ambassadors Tour once a week.

Visitor center. Shop. Cafe. Open Monday through Saturday 9:30 am to 4 pm, Sunday 12 noon to 4 pm, April through October. Ambassadors Tour must be booked ahead.

■ *Tomintoul*
Ballindalloch AB37 9AQ. 01907 590247
tomintoulwhisky.com

High on the lonely B9136 between Ballindalloch and the village of Tomintoul sits the Tomintoul distillery, built by a consortium of Glasgow blenders in 1964 and only the third new distillery to be built in Scotland in the 20th century.

The distillery, it has to be admitted, is far from pretty. Well let's face it, it's a couple of big industrial sheds really, with an admin block and a car park. But the village is fascinating and the setting is lonely, wild, and absolutely ravishing even (perhaps especially?) in bad weather. Actually it's so lonely and the weather is so changeable that according to legend the construction crew always had a fortnight's materials on site in case they got cut off by the weather. Presumably

Tomintoul

they had a fortnight's supply of food and drink as well, and perhaps a few good books, but history does not record.

Tomintoul was bought by Whyte & Mackay in 1973, and was considerably expanded; in 2000 it was sold on to the independent blender and bottler Angus Dundee, which three years later went on to buy Glencadam at Brechin as well.

Tours by appointment.

Keith

On Speyside's very eastern edge sits Keith, not one planned town but two. The medieval old town, around the 17th-century Auld Bridge over the Isla, goes back to the 12th century: its landmark, the **Milton Tower**, is the remaining portion of a late 15th-century fortified tower house. The main part of Keith to its east, though, was planned by the Earl of Findlater as early as 1750, and made its living out of water-powered textile mills. Fife Keith, a suburb on the west bank of the Isla, was built by Findlater's neighbor the Earl of Fife in 1817 to take advantage of the same water-power, and the Keith conurbation—if a town of some 4,500 people could be called a conurbation—was a center of the woolen industry right into the 1970s. Until a few years ago it even had a tartan museum with more than 500 examples of tartan going back to the 1720s. In fact the town was so associated with textile mills that its Strathisla distillery went by the name Milltown or Milton until 1951.

For the whisky tourist, therefore, Keith doesn't offer very much apart from Strathisla itself: The two main hotels, the **Royal** in Church Rd. and the **Grampian** in Regent Square, can each muster around 20 malts which would be something to boast about in an English pub but is no more than respectable here.

Don't write Keith off entirely, though, especially if the age of steam is your thing. The volunteer-run railway that links it with Dufftown has its HQ here: Shortly after the line was reopened the old railway station was rebuilt as faithfully as possible. It was declared open in 2003 and three years after that a museum was opened to go with it.

■ Glendronach
Forgue, Huntly AB54 6DB. 01466 730202
glendronachdistillery.co.uk

In a district notorious for small-scale unlicensed distilling, a consortium of local landowners came together in 1826—shortly after the legislation that made large-scale distilling a commercial prop-

[Glendronach] distillery itself is a handsome group of listed buildings nestling in a little glen… As well as being attractive it has the advantage of being easy to find and is very visitor friendly.

osition—to found their own legitimate concern in the grounds of a Georgian manor, Glen House. The group was headed by a colorful character named James Allardyce who popularized the whisky in Edinburgh, according to legend, by distributing free bottles to high-class prostitutes to share with their patrons. Word of mouth marketing indeed!

The distillery changed hands a number of times in the ensuing decades—for a while it belonged to a son of William Grant of Glenfiddich fame—and in 1960 was bought by William Teacher's. Like Ardmore, it was popular with blenders because its richness meant they only needed to use a little of it to give character to their neutral grain spirits; and this was precisely what Teacher's required. And like Ardmore, its direct-fired stills generated caramel, and the spirit was made even sweeter and richer through aging in sherry casks. The stills were the last in Scotland to be directly coal-fired, in fact, only switching to steam coils in 2005.

After Teacher's was sold to Allied Breweries in 1976 Glendronach had rather a torrid time, including a silent spell in the late 1990s. In 2008 it was bought by the same consortium of international financiers that owns Benriach in Speyside: Under their proprietorship the visitor center has been revamped and improved, and the whisky has been released in a huge variety of ages and expressions.

The distillery itself is a handsome group of listed buildings nestling in a little glen on the B9001 just off the A97 nine miles north of Huntly. As well as being attractive it has the advantage of being easy to find and is very visitor friendly.

Shop. Visitor center. Open 10 am to 4:30 pm, seven days, May through September; Monday through Friday, October through April. Five tours per day. Book ahead for Tasting Tours and Connoisseurs' Experience.

■ *Glenglassaugh*
Portsoy AB45 2SQ. 01261 842367
glenglassaugh.com

Founded in 1875, Glenglassaugh is a distillery that has risen from the dead... twice. It was originally established by a local businessman, James Moir, and inherited by his nephews when he

Glenglassaugh

died. But in 1892 one of them died too, and the survivor sold up to the newly formed Highland Distilleries. Fifteen years later Glenglassaugh was mothballed, and stayed that way for half a century. Parts of the site were used for other prurposes—the malting was an army bakery in World War II—but it wasn't until the returning prosperity and rising demand of the late 1950s that Highland moved back on to the site and completely rebuilt the distillery.

Sadly, the new plant couldn't turn out young spirit that met the requirements of the blenders for whom it was intended; and although the older single bottlings delighted connoisseurs, there wasn't enough money in it to keep the distillery alive. In 1986 it was closed again, this time for 22 years. Then in 2008 it was bought by a Dutch investment company that set about restoring it, inviting Scottish nationalist leader Alex Salmond to perform the first ceremonial mashing in in November of that year. The business survived at first on limited editions of very old stock and cheekily named bottling of new make (which can't be called whisky until it's three years old). In 2012 its first single malt, Revival, was launched at four years old, which includes a six-month finishing in sherry casks.

Visitor center. Shop. Cafe. Open Monday through Friday, April through October. Revival tours 10:15 am, 11:45 am, 1:15 pm, 2:45 pm. November to March Revival tours must be booked in advance. Behind The Scenes and Ultimate tours must also be booked ahead.

Knockdhu; photo © Reuben Paris

■ *Knockdhu*

Knock, Huntly AB54 7LJ. 01466 771223
ancnoc.com

Standing over 1,000 ft up on the slopes of the picturesque Knock Hills from which the distillery draws its water, Knockdhu's grey stone warehouse has something of the look of a hill fort on the northwest frontier and indeed, (and purely coincidentally) it did actually serve as a barracks for Indian troops during World War II.

Knockdhu was built in 1894 to supply malt for the Haig blend which was then starting its rise to superstardom, and has the distinction of being the only distillery that was actually built by rather than bought by the Distillers Company. Apart from that rather exotic spell as a barracks, it worked away unspectacularly until 1983 when it was one of several selected for the chop.

It was bought and reopened by Inver House Distillers in 1989 and is now once again working hard for its living. Very hard, in fact, since in its new incarnation it produces not mere fillings but a very distinguished bottled range under the AnCnoc umbrella—AnCnoc being Gaelic for Knock Hills. The AnCnoc family embraces possibly a wider selection of ages, finishes, expressions, vintages, special bottling, and limited editions than any other across the entire spectrum of characters from menacingly dark and peaty to light-bodied, summery, and lemony, making Knockdhu's tasting room the end point of every discerning whisky lover's tour of choice.

Knockdhu is nine miles from Keith on a side-road off the A95. *Tours by appointment.*

Strathisla

■ *Strathisla*

Seafield Avenue, Keith AB55 5BS. 01542 783044
maltwhiskydistilleries.com

Scotland's oldest operating distillery (and one of its prettiest), was founded by two local businessmen in a former mill on the banks of the Isla in 1786 in an attempt to exploit the 1784 Wash Act that reduced the duty levied on small-scale Highland distillers. The Act was a disaster and provoked a series of calamitous follow-up legislation culminating in the even more disastrous 1788 Lowland License Act after which the legislators withdrew, both bloodied and bowed, for 30 years.

Strathisla is the only survivor of Pitt the Elder's clumsy attempts at regulation: Its setting, its classic layout and small stills, and the way it has been carefully and sensitively extended over more than 200 years, make it a must-visit for whisky tourists both serious and casual. To add spice, it was at the center of a notorious post-war racket when a London financier named Pomeroy bought into William Longmore & Co., which had owned Strathisla since the 1820s, and started diverting supplies to the black market. The distillery, then known as Milton, was confiscated by the government and sold at auction in 1950, the successful bidder being Chivas Brothers with a bid of £71,000.

The visitor center with its luxurious Dram Room was opened in 1995 as a showcase for the Chivas Regal blend and its family of expressions, but Strathisla as a single is also available at 12 years old in the brown bottle in which it has been sold since the 1920s. It's hugely prized by connoisseurs and is often described as Scotland's best-kept secret.

Visitor center. Shop. Open Monday through Saturday, 9:30 am to 5 pm; Sunday 12 noon to 5 pm, April through October (last tour 4 pm); Monday through Friday, 9:30 am to 5 pm, November through March (shop only). Ultimate Chivas Experience and Straight from the Cask tours must be booked in advance.

Aberdeen

Britain's most northerly (and coldest) city in some ways resembles Edinburgh. Old Aberdeen, the 900-year-old burgh, is to the north of the modern city center and includes the medieval cathedral **St. Machar's**; but in the 18th century Aberdeen was dignified with many broad, elegant avenues, and in the 19th century these avenues were further ornamented with fine municipal and commercial buildings. All these different architectural layers survive because they were built of the extraordinarily durable local granite, which gives Aberdeen both its nicknames: The Granite City, and also the Silver City because of the grains of mica in the stone that sparkle and glitter in bright sunlight.

The city is the de facto capital of the most fertile and productive part of Scotland: The eastern seaboard and its hinterland, as in England, are the prime arable zones, producing mountains of barley for brewing and distilling. Aberdeen is practically besieged by distilleries and used to have some of its own: The last, Strathdee, closed in 1942. But its industrial base has always been fishing, shipbuilding, papermaking, textiles and, since the 1970s, North Sea oil and gas.

Nevertheless, Aberdeen still has much to offer the whisky lover. As a cosmopolitan city entertaining well-paid oil industry executives and engineers from all over the world, its hotel bars tend to be well-stocked with the pride of the region—the **Whisky Snug** at the Malmaison in Queens Rd. and the **Whisky Bar** at the Palm Court in Seafield Rd. are particularly well-regarded in this respect. Upmarket bars and restaurants also stock wider ranges than you would expect elsewhere: For instance, a dozen of them in the **Merchant Quarter** at the eastern end of Union Street have banded together to provide a "whisky walk" and stock 200 different whiskies between them. And the well-known **Prime Cuts** steak and lobster house in Crown Terrace, off Crown Street south of Union Street, has a wine bar upstairs—which is indeed called **Upstairs**—with an extensive selection.

Aberdeen's premier whisky bars, however, remain **The Grill** at 213 Union Street and **CASC** in Stirling Street. The Grill is an Edwardian mahogany delight opposite the **Music Hall**, which stocks some 450 malts and 50 "world whiskies" (and is conveniently close to the **Aberdeen Whisky Shop** at 474 Union Street where you can fill your shopping bag with anything from "entry level" malts to rare bottlings costing hundreds of pounds). CASC claims to pip The Grill with 500 whiskies; but at this stratospheric level, who's counting? CASC also stocks a handsome range of craft ales, a luscious variety of coffees, and genuine Cuban cigars, hence the name—Cigars, Ale, Scotch & Coffee… geddit? Oh, and locally distilled gins and spiced rum.

One last treat—on your way to Glengarioch be sure either to pause or indeed to book in at the **Meldrum House Hotel** in Oldmeldrum. This perfect miniature of a medieval Scottish castle is actually more oriented towards golf than whisky, but its 800-year-old **Cave Bar** stocks more than 100 malts including numerous unusual bottling of Glengarioch. The rest of the stock is largely supplied Gordon & MacPhail, so you just know there'll be some rare delights in there.

■ *Fettercairn*
Distillery Rd., Fettercairn, Laurencekirk AB30 1YE. 01561 340205
whyteandmackay.com

Fettercairn is the perfect example of how the landed gentry muscled in on distilling once they saw its potential. It grew out of an illicit distillery operated by a family named Guthrie in the Drumtochty Forest north of Fettercairn village, but almost as soon as the law had been changed in 1823 to make small-scale distilling unviable and large-scale distilling a good bet, Sir Alexander Ramsay of the Fasque Estate took over the operation and moved it down the hill into the village's old grain mill.

The Ramsays sold Fasque in 1829 to Sir John Gladstone, father of the future Prime Minister William Ewart Gladstone. It was run by a succession of managers and tenants until 1887, when it was burnt down. The family rebuilt it in the form you see today and ran it themselves until 1926, when it fell silent. It was to have been dismantled, but in 1939 it was sold to the owners of the Ben Nevis

Fettercairn

distillery and reopened. Today it belongs to Whyte & Mackay, and although it's off the main tourist routes it has had a shop and visitor center since 1989.

To find the attractively set distillery, with the Grampians as an impressive backdrop, get off the A90 Dundee-Aberdeen Road at Laurencekirk. Fettercairn is a couple of miles up the B9120.

Shop. Visitor center. Open from Easter through September, Monday through Saturday, 10 am to 4 pm.

■ Glengarioch
Distillery Rd., Oldmeldrum AB51 0ES. 01651 873450
glengarioch.com

Scotland's most easterly distillery is on the northern outskirts of Oldmeldrum, 14 miles north of Aberdeen on the A947 Banff Rd. It's also one of Scotland's most colorful, with not one but four creation myths and a 20-year dalliance with tomatoes behind it.

The orthodox version has it that the distillery was founded in 1797 by John and Alexander Manson and that their heirs had it until 1884, when they sold out to Leith wine shippers JG Thompson. Another story is that it was founded by Thomas Simpson, who sold it to Ingram Lamb & Co in 1827, who sold it to John Manson Jr.— who already owned another distillery in the town, Strathmeldrum—

in 1837. Version three is that the Mansons founded it in 1794 and sold it to Simpson who sold it to Ingram Lamb who sold it to John Manson Jr.... and to complicate matters still further, there's a mention of an earlier distillery from 1785, and in 1794 a local vicar wrote of "a distillery and brewery lately founded."

The visitor center at Glengarioch

If it all sounds a bit like the show *Dallas*, there is a serious point: Whisky in "the granary of Aberdeenshire" (as this district is known) in the late 18th century was no hole-and-corner affair. It was heavily capitalized and dealt in by serious businesspeople. In fact it was serious businesspeople very like the Mansons who drove the moonshiners out of business.

The tomatoes? Oh yes—Glengarioch changed hands (again!) in 1971 when Stanley P. Morrison bought it from DCL. Innovative, environmentally friendly, and conscious that energy prices were going through the roof, Morrison made the most of its gas bill by reusing waste heat to warm greenhouses. The venture lasted from 1973–1993 and was highly publicized, being featured by BBC's prime-time science and technology program *Tomorrow's World*, shortly before it became history.

In the same year that the greenhouses were closed, so was the maltings. It's now the visitor center.

Shop and visitor center open Monday through Saturday, 10 am to 4 pm. Standard tours at 11 am, 1 pm, 3 pm. Book ahead for groups, Wee Tasting tours, and VIP tours.

Glencadam

■ *Glencadam*
Smithfield Rd., Brechin DD9 7PA. 01356 622217
glencadamdistillery.co.uk

Glencadam is the last survivor of what used to be a clutch of distilleries in the ancient city—unchartered, but the seat of a Scottish Episcopalian bishop and therefore in the old sense a city—of Brechin.

A neat and compact complex of brownstone buildings overlooking the park, Glencadam looks more like a farm than a factory—which is hardly surprising, since before the distillery was built this northern outlier of Brechin was given over to market gardens on which the good burghers grew their own fruit and veg. The distillery was founded almost as soon as the 1823 Excise Act made it legal and was up and running by 1825; but the early bird in this case singularly failed to catch the worm. The founder, a Mr. Cooper, sold up after only two years and for the rest of the century Glencadam was run by a succession of short-lived tenants. It was closed and used as a barracks in both world wars, and stability only arrived in 1954 when it was bought by the Canadian drinks giant Hiram Walker.

Over the next 40 years Glencadam enjoyed considerable investment as its light, smooth spirit was a major component of the Ballantyne blends; but in 2000 it was declared surplus to requirements and closed. That wasn't to be the end of the story, though. Three years later it was bought by Angus Dundee, blender and bottler of Glasgow and London and already owner of Tomintoul on Speyside. Two years later the new owners launched the first official bottling of Glencadam, a 15-year-old; today various expressions are available from 10 to 21 years old.

Tours by appointment only, 2 pm to 4 pm, Monday through Thursday.

■ *Royal Lochnagar*

Balmoral, Crathie, Ballater AB35 5 TB. 01339 742700
discovering-distilleries.com

In a pretty wooded glen just off the B976 south of Crathie, 58 miles down the A93 from Aberdeen and in the imposing shadow of the 3,800-ft Lochnagar mountain, Royal Lochnagar is only a stone's throw from Balmoral as the crow flies… or rather, as the Queen and Prince Consort stroll.

For, only a few days after his royal neighbors had moved in, New Lochnagar Distillery proprietor John Begg dropped Prince Albert a note enquiring whether he might perhaps care for a look around. Begg was surprised, to put it mildly, when Albert turned up at the door the very next day with the Queen and a couple of royal offspring in tow to take advantage of the offer. Immediately the word "New" on the signboard was painted out and replaced with the word "Royal," and so it has remained.

Begg had built his distillery in 1845, taking advantage of the vicissitudes of fate that had stymied Robertson's distillery just across the Dee—built 1823, burned down by moonshiners in 1826, rebuilt, and burnt down again in 1841. Begg was also a pioneering blender who founded a major concern in Glasgow and whose name was a familiar brand to whisky drinkers until the 1970s. The distillery he founded, although one of the smallest in Scotland, has flourished since that royal visit in September 1848 and has been expanded several times, most recently in 1963. But the rebuildings have always been sympathetic and the place lives up to its surroundings. And being where it is, it's one of the most visited of Scotland's malt whisky distilleries, attracting more than 30,000 tourists a year.

Shop. Visitor center. Standard Tour, Family of Whisky Tour, Royal Tour. Check website for opening times. Always ring ahead to check availability/book.

Perth

The Scots love to give their cities nicknames—the Windy City, the Granite City, Auld Reekie, and so on—and Perth is known as the Fair City, because it is. But they might also have dubbed it the Ancient City, since it was the seat of the Pictish Kings of Alba as long ago as the 9th century and had probably been continuously inhabited for 5,000-odd years before that. Or they might equally have called it the Medieval Capital City, since its strategic location, its wealth, and its possession of the Stone of Scone made it a frequent resort of Scotland's kings.

In the late 18th century Perth became an industrial as well as a trading town, specializing in leather and linen manufacture—but not distilling. One distillery, Clockskerrie, later Isla, was installed in a former brewery at the eastern end of the Tay Bridge in 1851 and closed in 1926. But the whisky industry in Perth was more importantly the province of the great merchants such as Arthur Bell, John Dewar, and Matthew Gloag, blender of Famous Grouse, who bought their malts from the many distilleries in Perth's hinterland and sent it out into the world via Perth harbor.

The empires founded by these merchant princes have all been swallowed up by global combines now, and their headquarters have been moved far, far away. But for the whisky tourist there is one remaining solid link. At the **Bothie Perth** restaurant in Kinnoull Street there is a cocktail bar, the **Famous Grouse Bar,** which specializes in Famous Grouse variants and stablemates such as Highland Park from Orkney. That's because the Bothie used to be better known as Bordeaux House, HQ of Matthew Gloag & Sons. A wider—or at any rate less narrowly focused—range of 120+ malts and world whiskies is on offer at the magnificent **Edwardian Dickens Bar,** formerly the Central Bar, at 189 South Street, while handily close at 47 South Street **Exel Wines**, although primarily a wine merchant, has a better than respectable range of single and vatted malts, superior blends, and whisky liqueurs.

Daftmill

■ *Daftmill*

Collessie, near Cupar, Fife KY15 5RF. 01337 830303
daftmill.com

Hidden away down a farm track off the A91, just west of its junction with the A92 and four miles west of Cupar is Daftmill, so called because thanks to an optical illusion its millstream appears to run uphill, and, since 2005, home to one of the new crop of revivalist farm distilleries.

The Cuthbert family has been growing malting barley here for eight generations and decided to install a distillery in 2003 as part of the restoration of their handsome 150-year-old stone farm buildings. The venture has been as local an affair as the family could make it: The labor and materials were all local, apart from the copper stills; the barley is grown on the farm (and, in keeping with Lowland practice, is unpeated); the water comes from its own artesian well via a century-old water tower; and the spent grain goes to feed the family's beef herd.

The first spirit flowed from those Speyside-built stills in December 2005, and brothers Ian and Francis Cuthbert always vowed not to bottle it at less than 10 years old; at time of writing, though, the family has decided it isn't quite ready yet; so whisky lovers will just have to be patient for a little while longer!

Daftmill is still very much a working farm, so visits and tours are limited.

Tours by appointment only.

■ Eden Mill
Main Street, Guardbridge, St. Andrews, Fife KY19 0UU
01334 835038. edenmill.com

Eden Mill is unique among whisky distilleries in that it is also a working brewery. Unique, I hear you cry—surely every whisky distillery is also a brewery, since the wash from which the spirit is distilled is, to all intents and purposes, beer? Well, yes. But not many distilleries invite you to drink their wash—which is just as well, because it isn't very nice. Eden Mill, though, actually started out in life in 2012 as a brewery with a range including Shipwreck IPA, Seggie Porter, and The 19th Brew.

Founder Paul Miller then turned his hand to rectifying gin and came up with a variety of botanicals including sea buckthorn in his Original and Galaxy hops in his Hop Gin. The company seems to take endless delight in experimenting with botanicals; and in its distinctive earthenware swingtop bottles the ever-growing range has attracted a small army of devotees.

The whisky came later—the first new make went into cask only in April 2015, so it will be a while yet before it goes into bottle. But the same spirit of innovation that characterizes the range of gins will be there in the whisky too: As a former brewer himself, head distiller Scott Ferguson knows his malts and has been experimenting with additions of chocolate malt, crystal malt, and brown malt. He swears that flavors of shortbread and caramel have persisted through the process and are discernible in the immature spirit, so expect to be surprised.

Eden Mill's home is a bit unusual, too. From 1810 until 1890 it was a distillery known as The Seggie (hence the porter) belonging to one of the many branches of the Haig family. After that it was a papermill until 2008 when it finally closed and was bought by St. Andrew's University for conversion into industrial units and a green power-station. The severely utilitarian extension that houses the brewery/distillery is the opposite of picturesque, but if it's the liquid you're interested in rather than the architecture then this is the tour you must take.

Tours 11 am to 5 pm, seven days; ring ahead to secure a place. Private tours available most evenings; must be booked.

Glenturret; photo ©Fraser Band

■ *Glenturret*
The Hosh, Crieff PH7 4HA. 01764 656565
thefamousgrouse.com

The Hosh is a secluded little glen just outside Crieff which was reputed to be a hotbed of moonshining throughout the 18th century, with lookouts posted on the surrounding hills to warn of the approach of "gaugers" or excisemen. If that's the case then by 1775 the Drummond family, which farmed The Hosh, had built up a big enough trade to go legitimate and start paying their taxes—which is the story behind Glenturret's claim to be Scotland's oldest distillery.

The claim is disputed by some, though, not least because Glenturret closed in 1921, was stripped out in 1923, and spent the next 35 years as agricultural storage. It was rescued in 1957 by a whisky-loving entrepreneur, James Fairlie, who bought it, re-equipped it, built six new warehouses, and fired up the stills again in 1960. As sales director his son Peter turned it into one of Scotland's top 10 tourist attractions, building up annual visitor figures of 200,000+ from a base of zero. The rather dubious story of Towser the distillery cat's haul of 28,899 mice in 24 years dates from his period in charge and was a PR coup in 1987.

Glenturret has belonged to Highland Distillers of Famous Grouse fame since 1990 and its visitor centre is dubbed The Famous Grouse Experience. Hype aside, though, Glenturret is pretty much the archetype of the Highland malt distillery and for any whisky lover is a "must visit."

Visitor center. Shop. Restaurant. Open year-round, seven days: 10 am to 5 pm, November through February; 9 am to 6 pm, March through October.

Kingsbarns, Wemyss Room

■ *Kingsbarns*

East Newhall Farm, Kingsbarns, St. Andrews KY16 8QE.
01333 451300. kingsbarnsdistillery.com

Kingsbarns Links have long been famous as the home of one of the oldest golf clubs in the world, founded in 1793 and now closely associated with St. Andrews just seven miles up the A917 and Carnoustie further up the coast across the Firth of Tay. The links make up part of the enormous Cambo Estate, a magnet for well-heeled golfers ever since the lordly pile of Cambo House itself was transformed into a complex of luxury hotel rooms and self-catering apartments.

Now it's a magnet for whisky lovers, too, with the opening of Kingsbarns Distillery in a charming late 18th-century sandstone farmstead on the estate. The farm had long been derelict, but its traditional courtyard layout and distinctive Gothic revival crenellated dovecote (or doocot, as they call it round here) made it the ideal candidate for long and painstaking restoration.

Kingsbarns was conceived equally as a visitor attraction and working distillery. The first spirit flowed from the stills only in February 2015 and won't be released for sale until 2018 at the very earliest; but don't despair—your visit won't be dry of a dram since a major investor is the independent family-owned blender and bottler Wemyss Malts, whose own range stocks the shop handsomely.

Shop. Café. Four grades of tour available year round. Book ahead online or by phone.

■ Strathearn

Bachilton Farm Steading, Methven PH1 3QX. 01738 840100
strathearndistillery.com

One of the newest—and by its own account, the smallest—of Scottish distilleries is Strathearn in Methven, just a few miles west of Perth on the A85. Strathearn shares the former farm buildings at Bachilton with a team-building firm, BlueSky Enterprises, which is how owner Tony Reeman-Clark and distillery manager Stuart McMillan met—Stuart was actually working for BlueSky while Tony was a client.

Tony, a systems manager and whisky fanatic, had already taken the three-day distilling course that used to be run at Bladnoch and the two decided to take over the rest of the buildings in the farmyard and set up on their own. As with many craft whisky distillers their first product was actually a gin—or rather a range of gins, one of which (Heather Rose) turns pink when water is added. Their first whisky ran from the 500-liter spirit still, Wee Erin, in October 2013 and is currently aging in 50-liter casks (called "octaves" in the trade).

Everything is miniature here, not just the still and the casks—even the new make is having its 28-day maturation in 30-litre casks

Everything is miniature here [Strathearn], not just the still and the casks—even the new make is having its 28-day maturation in 30-litre casks made variously of cherrywood, chestnut, and mulberry.

made variously of cherrywood, chestnut, and mulberry. The purpose is twofold: First, to recreate the methods and materials of the 18th century, when small distillers had to be able to pack up and run at a moment's notice; second, to allow themselves the craft distiller's prerogative of small-scale experiments which won't break the bank if they don't quite work. The longer-term plan is to create small batches using peated and unpeated malts, aged and finished in all sorts of casks.

Any one of the team will gladly show you round, provided you book well in advance; but Methven is not really on the tourist trail and the real visitor experience at Strathearn is rather more intense than a mere guided tour. It runs one, three, and five-day gin and whisky-making courses that have attracted nascent craft distillers from all over Britain and Europe.

Tours by arrangement, 10 am to 4 pm, Monday through Friday. Must be booked ahead. Whisky and gin courses £65–£840.

■ *Tullibardine*
Stirling Street, Blackford PH4 1QG. 01764 682252
tullibardine.com

It's got a bit of history, Tullibardine—which is weird, as it was only established in 1949. But the derelict buildings which the distinguished Welsh-born distillery engineer William Delmé-Evans (also responsible for Jura and Glenallachie) saw and thought ripe for conversion had previously been a brewery, and it's always said that it was from a predecessor on the site that James IV ordered the brews for his coronation at Scone in 1488. Hence the significance of the number in Tullibardine's branding.

Delmé-Evans sold Tullibardine in 1953 and through a series of corporate takeovers it ended up in the hands of Whyte & Mackay, which didn't really want it and closed it in 1995. Eight years later a consortium of whisky-loving businessmen bought it for a knockdown price and reopened it, intending to make it as much a tourist attraction as a working distillery—hence the upmarket shopping mall on part of the site.

And Tullibardine, if not especially picturesque, is eminently visitable. Not only is it both well-located and easy to find (Blackford is just off the A9 halfway between Perth and Stirling and not all

Tullibardine casks

that far from Gleneagles), but Delmé-Evans's one-room layout also makes a brilliant interpretation center, presenting the whole process in a way that's easy to see, digest, and comprehend.

Visitor center. Shop. Cafe. Open year-round Monday through Saturday, 9:30 am to 5 pm; Sunday, 10 am to 5 pm. Four levels of tour: Standard tours on the hour, 10 am to 4 pm. Prior booking essential.

Pitlochry

Pitlochry scarcely existed until Queen Victoria made the Highlands fashionable in the 1840s, and once the railway arrived in 1863 it became one of the most popular tourist resorts in Scotland. It still is, and in summer the resident population of 2,500 is completely overwhelmed.

Which means, of course, that there is more to see or do in and around Pitlochry—apart from visiting its three very different distilleries—than anyone could hope to pack into a two-week holiday. You don't even need your car, since the station escaped Dr. Beeching's axe and most of the attractions are within easy walking distance of the town center. Walking distance in the Highlands, mind, is a rather elastic concept—over 40 miles of walks start from the town center, some easy, some impossible, and all through enchanting scenery of woods, lochs, and hills.

If the thought of all that walking makes you hungry, drop into **MacDonald's**. It does burgers—but not Big Macs or quarter-pounders with cheese. In fact it's one of many independent restaurants in town ranging from budget to gourmet and like most of them, it has a pretty impressive range of malt whiskies. **Mackay's**, with a choice of 120 and counting, is the town's best-known whisky bar, but many of the local hotels sport a good selection too, notably the **Tummel Inn** near the Queen's View and the astonishing Victorian mock-baronial pile that is the **Atholl Palace Spa Hotel**.

And if you want a few souvenirs, Pitlochry is absurdly well-provided with whisky shops for such a small town. They include a branch of **The Whisky Shop**; **Drinkmonger**, which is actually a branch of Royal Mile Whiskies; and the legendary local independent **Robertson's**, all of them on Atholl Rd. which is Pitlochry's high street.

Aberfeldy

■ *Aberfeldy*

Aberfeldy PH15 2EB. 01887 822010
dewars.com

Beautifully set among the wooded slopes of the Tay valley, Aberfeldy is a rather grand, formal building that could be the barracks of a distinguished Highland regiment if it weren't for the tell-tale pagoda topping the old maltings. And its grandness is well-deserved, since it occupied an important place in the global development of the whisky industry in the early 20th century.

The distillery was built in 1898 by John Alexander Dewar and Tommy Dewar, sons of Perth wine and spirit merchant John Dewar. Dewar had set up in business in 1846 and became an enthusiastic disciple of the new art of blending. After his death in 1880 his sons first leased a distillery and then built their own, here in the village where their father had been born. While John Alexander was the cool head, Tommy was a forward-looking marketer who was the first to advertise alcohol in the cinema and the first to invite film cameras into the distillery to make a (silent) documentary about it. He also tackled the export markets, visiting 26 countries in two years to make Dewar's one of the world's biggest brands. He became an MP in 1900 and, in 1919, Baron Dewar. By the time Dewar's was taken over by the Distillers Company in 1925 it owned seven distilleries.

Easy to find—it's 33 miles from Perth up the A9 and A827—Aberfeldy is a popular attraction with a state-of-the-art visitor center in the old maltings.

Visitor center. Shop. Café. Four levels of tour. Open Monday through Saturday, 10 am to 4 pm, November through March; Monday through Saturday, 10 am to 6 pm, and Sunday, 12 noon to 4 pm, April through October.

■ *Blair Athol*

Perth Rd., Pitlochry PH16 5LY. 01796 482003
discovering-distilleries.com

A picture-postcard group of attractive stone buildings set round a pleasant courtyard, Blair Athol (NOT in the village of the same name, but on the outskirts of Pitlochry) is one of Diageo's flagship distilleries and is also a very popular visitor attraction.

First founded in 1798 by two local entrepreneurs named Robertson and Stewart, it quickly proved a failure but was reopened in 1825, almost immediately after the 1823 Excise Act. It coasted along, going through many changes of ownership, until 1932 when the Great Depression caught up with it and it closed. The very next year it was bought by the Perth blender and bottler Arthur Bell, but remained in mothballs until after the war.

Blair Athol; photo © Tom Cockram

Once it was back in action, Blair Athol was selected for heavy investment: Its capacity was doubled in the 1970s and in the 1980s, when Bell's was becoming Britain's best-selling whisky, it was opened to visitors. Not everyone approved—serious whisky connoisseurs were very sniffy and stayed away in droves—but the public loved it and soon it was attracting 30,000 tourists a year. Since then it has gone from strength to strength, offering four levels of tour from the standard to the Allt Dour (Blai Athol's original name) Deluxe.

Shop. Tours 10 am to 4 pm, Monday through Saturday, November through March; 10 am to 6 pm, Monday through Saturday, 12 noon to 4 pm, Sunday, April through October. Book premium tours in advance.

Dallwhinnie; photo courtesy of Diageo

■ *Dalwhinnie*
Dalwhinnie PH19 1AB. 01540 672219
discovering-distilleries.com

Of all the ill-omened start-ups in business history, Dalwhinnie's must rank among the most disastrous. Its location, over 1,000 feet up on a mountain pass roughly equidistant from Perth and Inverness, in officially the coldest place in Scotland, was scarcely promising; and the consortium that had borrowed £10,000 to build it in 1897 went bust before it was finished.

The distillery—originally called Strathspey—was quickly sold to new owners who changed its name, perhaps to banish ill-luck; but they fared little better and in 1905 Dalwhinnie was auctioned for just £1,250 to an American firm, Cook & Bernheimer. Not long after that Prohibition came along and the Americans quickly unloaded their unwanted purchase on to a Scottish firm, which promptly sold out to the Distillers Company.

Had enough? Wait! The distillery was burnt to the ground in 1934, the rebuilding took until 1938, and in 1940 it went silent for the duration of World War II.

One reason why Dalwhinnie kept getting another chance was that the whisky was always so highly rated. Another was its magnificent setting: It's the joint highest in Scotland along with Braeval, and commands astonishing views of the Cairngorms to the east and the Monadhliath range to the north. And although it's a long way from anywhere, the A9 goes right past the front door (as indeed does the Highland Railway: Dalwhinnie still has a station, although the distillery's own sidings were axed in 1969), bringing around 50,000 visitors a year.

Visitors center. Shop. Four levels of tour and tasting including chocolate pairing. Tasting-only option. Open seven days year-round except December 25–27 and January 1–2. Check website or call for opening times.

■ *Edradour*

Balnauld, Pitlochry PH16 5JP. 01796 472095
edradour.com

Pitlochry's second malt distillery (off the A924 just to the east of the town) is also Scotland's smallest—or was, until Loch Ewe stole its crown—and is in many respects its most interesting.

It's of the same vintage as its much, much, bigger neighbor; but unlike Blair Athol it wasn't founded by a landowner seeking to cash in on the 1823 Excise Act but by a consortium of local small farmers anxious to maintain their own domestic supply. Its still is only just big enough to be legal under the terms of the Act, and the complex of whitewashed buildings housing all the various processes looks more like a cluster of cottages than a factory. For an idea of scale, Edradour mashes just a ton of malt a week, while Blair Athol mashes over 80 tons.

Edradour

The farmers' co-op went commercial when it founded a company in 1841; in 1922 the company was bought by an American distiller, JG Turney, whose principal shareholder was leading New York Mafioso Jack Costello, dubbed the Prime Minister of Crime. A lot of Edradour was doubtless enjoyed by the men in flash suits!

More recently Edradour was bought by Campbell distillers, Scottish subsidiary of Pernod Ricard. Then in 2002 Pernod declared its intention to close the distillery, but instead sold it to independent blender and bottler Signatory Vintages of Edinburgh. Despite or perhaps because of its size it has become one of the most-visited distilleries in Scotland, and given its setting in the glen of the eponymous burn, with spectacular Highland views all around, you'll understand why when you make your own pilgrimage.

Shop. Visitor center. Tours on the hour (last tour one hour before closing). Open Monday through Saturday, 10 am to 4 pm, November through February; Monday through Saturday, 10 am to 4 pm, and Sunday 12 noon to 4 pm, March through April; Monday through Saturday, 10 am to 5 pm, and Sunday 12 noon to 5 pm, May through October. Groups of 8+ book ahead.

Edinburgh

As a tourist destination, Edinburgh needs no introduction. Arguably Britain's most beautiful city—and possibly one of the most beautiful in the world—Edinburgh's great glory is that when the developers of the Georgian era seized upon it they built an entirely new town rather than tearing down the winding streets and quaint buildings of the old. Simply by crossing a railway bridge you can move within minutes from spacious squares and elegant boulevards to Britain's best-preserved and most extensive medieval townscape—and as a bonus, the historic city center escaped the Blitz virtually unscathed.

Edinburgh is also, of course, home to the **Edinburgh Art Festival,** the world's most celebrated arts festival. In August, every space that can claim to be a venue hosts a show of some sort and the streets pullulate with visitors. But what does it have to offer the whisky lover?

Not, unfortunately, a malt distillery. In Gorgie on the city's western outskirts is the North British grain distillery, one of the country's leading makers of neutral spirit for blending (and for vodka!). But for malt lovers Edinburgh is a center of consumption, not production. The multiplicity of single malts in various styles, ages, and strengths available in the city beggars belief.

Before diving into shopping it might be as well to enjoy a little education, and you can come leave the **Scotch Whisky Experience** (scotchwhiskyexperience.co.uk) on Castle Hill at the very top of the Royal Mile feeling you know everything there is to know. Opened in May 1988 in an imposing Victorian school building, the place is absolutely huge—as well it might be: The centerpiece is a barrel-ride rather similar to the one at the Viking Experience in York, which glides you round a replica distillery explaining the finer points of making and maturing malt whisky as you go. There are functions rooms and corporate hospitality suites too, and in the castle Hill Room you can even get married!

On top of its heritage and entertainment functions, the Scotch Whisky Experience runs some pretty heavyweight educational events such as the **Morning Masterclass** and the **Sense of Scotland** tasting tutorials. These are all great fun and highly informative for the civilian whisky lover, but they are more than that, too: The certificate issued at the end is recognized by the Scotch Whisky Association, and the courses are attended by trade and industry students as well as tourists. If only school had been this educational! To round it off you can see the world's biggest collection of whiskies—currently 3,500 bottles—experience the best of Scottish produce and cooking in the **Amber Restaurant**, and then start your shopping bonanza.

Just about every department store, gift shop and supermarket in Edinburgh stocks a wide range of malts, but for the enthusiast it's the specialist shops that are the prize. The Scotch Whisky Experience itself has a pretty impressive shop with more than 300 whiskies—blends and grains as well as malts—and all sorts of interactive gadgetry to help you make your selection if you're overwhelmed by choice. But if you feel brave enough to risk an even more bewildering shopping experience, there are two whisky shops within a stone's throw of the Scotch Whisky Experience— the **Whiski Rooms** in North Bank Street round to your left from the end of Castle Hill, and **The Whisky Shop** in Victoria Street to your right. A little further down the Royal Mile, in the High Street, is **Royal Mile Whiskies**; but don't fill your shopping trolley until you've gone a couple of hundreds further down to **Cadenhead's** in Canongate. Cadenhead's is primarily an independent bottler, under the same ownership as the Springbank distillery in Campbeltown, and its shop, though not huge, is fantastic and you'll be stunned by the range of specialist bottlings on display. In the New Town there's another branch of The Whisky Shop in the mall in Prince's Street.

After all that shopping you'll need a drink—a whisky, perhaps. A number of pubs have gathered themselves under the Whisky Bars of Edinburgh banner, pledging to offer a huge selection. They include the **Black Cat** and **Abbotsford Bar**, both in Rose Street; Whiski Bar and the **Albanach**, High Street; **Bow Bar**, West Bow; **Leslie's**, Ratcliffe Terrace; **Teuchter's**, William Street; **Stockbridge Tap**, Raeburn Place; **Thomson's**, Morrison Street; and the **Whiski Rooms**. But as you would expect, the city has plenty more watering-holes where the selection of whiskies will surprise and delight you: The **Canny Man's**, Morningside; the **Devil's Advocate**, Advocate Close; the **Cafe Royal**, West Register Street; the **Balmoral Hotel,** Prince's Street; **Usquabae at Ryan's Bar**, Hope Street; and quite probably the nearest pub to wherever you happen to be standing.

Glenkinchie; photo courtesy of Diageo

■ *Glenkinchie*

Peastonbank, Pencaitland, EH34 5ET. 01875 342004
discovering-distilleries.com

A mere 20 miles from Edinburgh city center, Glenkinchie is set in an attractive glen in the hamlet of Peastonbank two miles south of Pencaitland, from which it is signposted. It's not actually too hard to find, and is well worth the effort.

The distillery was first licensed in 1837 by local farmers John and George Rate, although it's suspected that they had been operating for some time before that. They ran it until 1859 before converting it into a sawmill. But in 1890, with phylloxera ravaging the vineyards of France and severely curtailing the world's supply of Cognac, a consortium of Edinburgh businessmen stepped in and reopened it, installing the two largest stills in Scotland. Apart from a brief closure during World War I when barley was short, it's been thriving ever since.

The old maltings were closed in 1968 and have been converted into an award-winning visitor center and museum whose center-piece is a scale model of a distillery made for the Empire Exhibition in Wembley in 1925. A shuttle bus runs direct from Edinburgh city center to the distillery three times a day.

Shop. Visitor center. Standard tours or Flavour of Scotland tours (with comparative tasting) seven days, until 2 pm, November through March; until 3 pm, April through October. Ring to book.

Malt fork at Glengarioch

PART IV:

Gin, Vodka, & Rum Distilleries

It's a little-known fact that since the giant Gordon's Distillery at Laindon in Essex, South-east England, closed in 1998 and production of Gordon's and Tanqueray gins and Smirnoff vodka was transferred to Cameronbridge, Scotland has at least equalled, if not exceeded, England's production of white spirits. For although England still has important gin and vodka distilleries including Greenall's, Beefeater, Plymouth, and Bombay Sapphire, Scotland boasts two of the largest column stills in the world in Cameronbridge and William Grant's plant at Girvan.

These giants, however, are not Scotland's only producers of gin and vodka, for the same fervor for craft-made white spirits that has swept England in the last 20 years has not passed Scotland by. Strathleven of Dumbarton, founded in 2006, led the charge with Valt Vodka; and since then small-scale gin and vodka distilleries have proliferated with a variety of business models, motivations, and types of product. Among the "new" gin distilleries are two very well known and old-established names in malt whisky, Bruichladdich on Islay with The Botanist, and Balmenach in Speyside (one of Scotland's oldest distilleries but sadly not open to the public) with Caorunn. Others include minute craft operations buried deep in the woods, lifestyle enterprises in picture-postcard seaside cottages, and swinging style bars in the throbbing heart of the city. Few of them (apart, obviously, from the bars) are really geared up for visitors; but you never know.

■ *Crossbill*

Inshriach Estate, Aviemore PH22 1QS. 07515 68396
jonathan@CrossbillGin.com. crossbillgin.com

Perhaps Britain's strangest distillery, Crossbill was founded by former architect Jonathan Engels in 2010 in a row of old chicken sheds in the Cairngorm Forest. Although only in his early 30s, Engels had already launched a contract-made flavored vodka, Pincer, which is infused with wild elderflower and milk thistle,

Crossbill was founded by former architect Jonathan Engels in 2010 in a row of old chicken sheds in the Cairngorm Forest.

and was encouraged by its success to go one further and build h
own distillery.

The choice of site was determined by the proximity of
plantation of native juniper, one of only two botanicals Jonatha
uses (the other is rosehip, also locally gathered); but its idiosyncra
has done the brand no harm in terms of awareness: In fact it wo
Channel 4's Shed of the Year 2015 competition out of 2,000 entrie
It's unheated, so on very cold days the Crosby gin-still is wrappe
up in a customized tweed jacket; the other sheds in the row ar
adorned with antique signs proclaiming them to be the Residen
Bar, the Ladies' Waiting Room, and the General Store (also know
as the Inconvenience Store, as it has no liquor license). There ma
or may not be a Gin Shed Festival every Easter.

Visit? Well, you might get a tour if you're staying on the esta
Which you might well want to do: Crossbill is far from being the onl
eccentricity you'll find there.

■ Dark Matter

Burn o' Bennie Rd., Banchory, Aberdeen AB31 5NN. 01330 822339
info@darkmatterdistillers.com. darkmatterdistillers.com

Scotland's first and so far only rum distillery was founded afte
a holiday in the Dominican Republic in 2011 when Jim McEwen
found that none of the island's distilleries ran tours. "It would be
easier," he reflected, "to build your own." Back home, that's wha
he and brother John did, recruiting Heriot-Watt graduate and re
searcher Cory Mason as their master distiller.

After many setbacks including a failed attempt at finding inves
tors, production started in April 2015 on a custom-designed copper
column still. Dark Matter's first product is an intensely spicy rum
made from clarified refinery-grade molasses, mashed with an ad
dition of pot ale like sourdough-mashed Bourbon, and fermented
with a local strain of yeast. A pot still is on its way to Banchory, so
the McEwens can add an oak-aged rum to the range.

■ Dunnet Bay

Dunnet, Thurso, Caithness KW14 8XD. 01847 851287
info@dunnetbaydistillers.co.uk. dunnetbaydistillers.co.uk

Perhaps because it's such an expensive industry to set up in, small-scale distilling hasn't attracted very many of what are termed lifestyle entrepreneurs:" that is, people who see their business as supporting the way they want to live rather than dictating it and often as much an ideological construct as a commercial one.

For Martin and Claire Murray, though, establishing the Dunnet Bay distillery near Thurso in their native Caithness has been as much a labor of love as a business decision.

In 2012 Martin, a chemical engineer in the oil industry, Claire, a tourism and hospitality graduate, and their young and growing family faced a critical decision. They were living in France but yearning for the north of Scotland, when Martin's employers asked him to move to Nigeria. Instead, they returned to Claire's home town, Dunnet, where they fulfilled a long-held ambition to set up their own gin distillery using locally foraged botanicals. So in Dunnet Bay's Rock Rose gin you'll find rose root (which was apparently highly prized by the Vikings who once ruled here), rowanberry, blueberry, and sea buckthorn.

John hadn't give up working as an oil industry consultant when this book went to press, but every batch the Murrays have produced has sold out straight away; and with newcomers Rock Rose Navy Strength and Holy Grass Vodka meeting enthusiastic welcomes, surely it can't be long.

The distillery is open to visitors during the summer months— always ring ahead for opening times and tour details.

■ Edinburgh Gin Distillery

1a Rutland Place, Edinburgh EH1 2AD. 0131 656 2810
info@edinburghgindistillery.com. edinburghgindistillery.co.uk

Boutique distillery bars haven't quite caught on in the UK as they have in the states: London, not surprisingly, has a couple, and since 2014 Edinburgh has had one too.

Based at a former farm (which was itself a distillery throughout the 19th century) in Inverkeithing at the northern end of the Forth Road Bridge from Edinburgh, Spencerfield Spirits was founded in 2005 by former Glenmorangie marketing director Alex Nicol and his partner Jane Eastwood to acquire and develop two rather interesting whiskies from Whyte & Mackay. The Sheep Dip blend had been launched in 1974 by a Gloucestershire farmer and publican, a Mr.

Top—Mini stills set up for a Gin Making Experience at the Edinburgh Gin Distillery. Visitors have the opportunity to make their own gin over a 3-hour experience.

Bottom—The Heads and Tales cocktail bar with Edinburgh Gin's stills— Caledonia and Flora in the background.
Photos courtesy of Edinburgh Gin.

Dowdeswell, as an innovation—a gimmick, some traditionalists said—in a market that was seeing precious little innovation at the time. Pig's Nose, a blended malt, followed three years later. In due course Mr. Dowdeswell sold the brands to Invergordon, which in 1993 was bought by Whyte & Mackay. Despite the names, the two brands are deadly serious: Sheep Dip has a 40% malt content, while Pig's Nose includes 8- and 12-year-old malts.

While at Glenmorangie Mr. Nicol had pioneered cask finishing, and Spencerfield's next whisky launch, The Feathery, was a blended malt finished in sherry casks. In the meantime Spencerfield had branched out, having Edinburgh Original Gin contract-distilled in Birmingham in 2010. In 2014 the brand found a home of its own when two small stills, Flora and Caledonia, were installed in the Head & Tales Bar in the basement of the Rutland Hotel in the very shadow of Edinburgh Castle. A new brand, Cannonball Navy Gin, was added to the Original as were a range of gin-based liqueurs.

Customers can enjoy the Spencerfield's products, among many others, by night, but by day the stills are the stars, with talks, tours and tastings at £10 and £25 and the three-hour Gin Making Experience at £75, for which you also get a bottle of the gin you designed.

■ NB (North Berwick)

15 St. Andrew St. N. Berwick EH39 4NU. 0845 4674547
info@nbgin.co.uk. nbgin.com

North Berwick was officially founded in 2013 by lawyers Steve and Viv Muir, who wanted to set up a business of their own—but definitely not in the law! They started out planning to open a brewery, but then decided that their common passion was gin. They experimented with botanicals in their kitchen for quite some time—first using a contraption made out of a pressure-cooker, then on a proper (and fully licensed!) table-top still—before arriving at their ideal grist and the optimum addition regime to produce a classic London Dry. They now operate from a unit on an industrial estate, using a custom-made gin still from long-established gin still maker, John Dore, and to their 42% abv Classic London Dry, have added a Navy Gin at 57% and a citrus vodka. Sadly, the distillery is not open to the public.

■ *Ogilvy Spirits*

Hatton of Ogilvy Farm, Glamis, Forfar DD8 1UH
ogilvyspirits.com

Graeme and Caroline Jarron decided to start distilling their own potato vodka as a way of diversification on the farm their family has worked since 1910. Graeme started work on the stillhouse in early 2014 and finished it in the summer of that year. With the help of Heriot Watt-trained master distiller Abhi Banek a custom-made John Dore still was installed over the winter, and the first Ogilvy Potato Vodka was produced in early 2015.

Sadly the distillery isn't open to the public, which is a shame because it has many points of interest. It's one of a handful of Scottish distilleries—artisanal or mainstream—where the entire process of growing the raw materials to bottling the finished product is carried out on site, and a particular point of interest is that the still is heated by solar electricity, also "made" on site.

However, with Glamis Castle and other tourist attractions only a stone's throw away, Graeme's mum Grace has one double en-suite letting room at the farmhouse. Surely a pleasant and polite enough guest would be allowed a sneaky peek at the distillery? Phone 01307 840229 to book!

■ *Shetland*

Saxa Vord, Unst, Shetland ZE2 9EF. 01957 711711
stuart@shetlandreelgin.com. shetlandreelgin.com

Saxa Vord on the Shetland isle of Unst is very nearly at the northernmost tip of the UK and getting there is quite a trek involving a flight, a hire-car, and two ferry trips. But this being Scotland (or is it? Shetland is far more Viking than Scots), you'll find a warm welcome once you get there. For here, on a former Royal Air Force base, you'll find a holiday resort with Britain's most northerly brewery (Valhalla) almost next door and Britain's most northerly distillery right on site.

Founded in 2014 by whisky industry consultant Stuart Nickerson and his wife Wilma, the Shetland Distillery Company currently produces its own Shetland Reel small-batch gin whose botanicals include local applemint. A whisky still is to be added in due course but in the meantime the company is bottling different expressions of Glenglassaugh—rescued from closure—under the name Shetland Reel whisky. Saxa Vord has self-catering and hostel accommodation as well as a restaurant and bar, and the distillery includes a tasting room for visitors (welcome, but by appointment).

■ *Summerhall Distillery*

Summerhall, Causewayside, Edinburgh EH9 1PL. 0131 290 2901
enquiries@pickeringsgin.com. pickeringsgin.com

The Summerhall arts complex just south of Edinburgh's Old Town and in the shadow of Arthur's Seat must surely be the most impressive home a craft gin distillery could ask for. Built in 1914–1925 to house the Royal School of Veterinary Studies (universally known as the Old Dick after its founder William Dick), it was vacated in favor of a more modern out-of-town campus in 2011 and instead of being demolished was converted into a warren of artists' studios, performance and exhibition spaces, and artisans' workshops—one of the latter being Summerhall Distillery.

Founded in 2013 by builder and engineer Matt Gammell and former butler and mixologist Marcus Pickering, the distillery occupies the old animal hospital's kennels. Pickering's Gin is unusual in that the still, Gert, is heated not by direct flame or steam coils but by a bain-marie affair so the neutral spirit and botanicals, which were adapted from a handwritten 1947 recipe supposedly found in a coat pocket, are simmered gently together in uniform heat.

Right next door to the distillery is the complex's pub, the Royal Dick (once the small animal infirmary), into which Pickering's Gin is actually piped. Also on draught are ales from Barney's Brewery, which occupies the oldest part of the site where in the 18th century there stood… a brewery!

Distillery tours are available at £10 a head at 2:30 pm and 4 pm, Monday through Friday, and 1 pm, 2:30 pm, and 4 pm Saturdays.

APPENDIX I
Speyside

Ballindalloch Castle

With 46 distilleries packed in and around a valley no more than 40 miles long, Speyside is the most concentrated spirit-producing region in Scotland and is second only to Cognac, France in terms of distilleries per square mile. The district has almost the perfect conditions for whisky production: The surrounding hills provide both pure spring water—of which distillers use an awful lot—and a degree of shelter from the worst of the weather; the valley floor and lower slopes are good arable land for barley production; there has historically been plenty of the peat required to turn all that barley into malt; and the railway down the valley to the North Sea ports made for efficient low-cost transport of the finished product. During boom times Speyside has always, therefore, been the first region to attract new investors, while in bad times the rate of attrition has been slower than in other parts.

If Speyside is all about distilling, so is its tourism. The surrounding hills are not as thickly studded with aerial zipwires, mountain-biking tracks, and other outdoor sports centers as most other parts of Scotland. **Ballindalloch Castle**, the Pearl of the North, is stunningly beautiful; but Speyside is no Deeside, and Ballindalloch is possibly the only attraction of any size in the upper and middle reaches of the valley that is not directly related to whisky—although even Ballindalloch now has its own craft distillery in a restored farmstead on the estate.

So it's whisky that brings tourists flocking to Speyside and the group of charming towns in its lower reach—Elgin, Rothes, Dufftown, Aberlour and, somewhat off to the east, Keith. Which makes it all the stranger that only a dozen of the 46 distilleries should be regularly open to visitors. That dozen, though, includes some of the greatest names in whisky. For the convenience of the tourist, seven of them are linked on a circuit known as the **Malt Whisky Trail** and marked out with brown roadsigns: The recommended itinerary starts at The Glenlivet right up in the wilds, descends to Cardhu at Ballindalloch, then to Glenfiddich, Glen

> Speyside Cooperage is the last place in Britain where you can still see a dedicated working cooperage of any size.

Grant, Strath Isla, and Glen Moray, and ends at Benromach in Forres, one of the region's smallest distilleries and almost beside the seaside. The trail doesn't add up to all that many miles; for obvious reasons, though, motorists are advised to take three days over completing the entire circuit!

There are two stops on the Malt Whisky Trail that aren't working distilleries, and the first of them is a living reminder of the allied trades that once supported the business of making whisky. Whisky is nothing without oak casks to age in, and while **Speyside Cooperage** (Craigellachie AB38 9RS. 01340 871108. speysidecooperage.co.uk) isn't quite the last in Scotland, it is the last manufacturer of oak casks on any scale. A handful of distilleries still have a cooperage, but mainly engaged in repair and maintenance: Like them, Speyside Cooperage repairs and refurbishes but also makes over 100,000 new hogsheads, butts, casks and puncheons a year. The coopers here still use traditional instruments, beveling the staves with old-fashioned spokeshaves, bashing down the hot iron hoops with hammers and chisels, and judging their work entirely by eye. There was a time when any liquid that travelled did so in a barrel, and every town had its cooperages—in Burton-on-Trent there were once more coopers than brewers—and Speyside Cooperage is the last place in Britain where you can still see a dedicated working cooperage of any size. (The Burgundian parent company, Tonnellerie François Frères, also has a site at Broxburn in central Scotland which isn't open to the public). Speyside Cooperage's Acorn to Cask exhibition is open year-round, Monday through Friday, 9 am to 4 pm (last tour 3:30 pm), and there's also a shop and cafe.

The second of these—and the last stop on the recommended itinerary—was a working distillery from 1898 until 1983, when it was included in the great Distillers Company cull. **Dallas Dhu in Forres** was one of the last distilleries to be designed by Charles Doig before the great crash of 1900 when Pattison Brothers, one of Scotland's biggest blenders and bottlers, went bust owing its suppliers hundreds of thousands of pounds. It changed ownership many times in its early years, ending up in the hands of the Distillers Company in 1929. Despite two long silences—1930–1936 and 1939–1947—its malt was acclaimed as one of Speyside's true greats and there was dismay when it figured on the 1983 hit-list. But, said DCL, Dallas Dhu's uncertain water supply had doomed it, and so it closed. Then in 1988 it was bought, still more or less intact, by Historic Scotland to be converted into a museum of whisky. It's a great opportunity to examine the workings of a distillery, to poke your head into all the various vessels, and to gain an understanding of the whole process without being interrupted by people actually trying to make whisky. In fact it might be more logical—especially if you've never visited a distillery before—to start at Dallas Dhu and do the whole trail backwards. That way you'd end up at The Glenlivet, which might be no bad thing! Dallas Dhu (Manachie Road, Forres IV36 2RR. 01309 676548. historic-scotland.gov. uk) is open seven days a week, 9:30 am to 5:30 pm, April through September, and Saturday through Wednesday, 9:30 am to 4:30 pm, November through March.

If fewer than a third of Speyside's distilleries are regularly open to the public, there's one time of year when almost all of them hang out the welcome sign; and that's during the **Spirit of Speyside Malt Whisky Festival** (spiritofspeyside.com) at the end of every April.

The Festival has been running since 1999 and was originally conceived by industry leaders, local businesspeople, and tourism professionals as a way of extending the season into the "shoulder month" of April, mainly by allowing tourists into distilleries that were normally forbidden territory to the general public. But whisky is so deeply embedded not just in the economy but in the culture, the art, the very life of Speyside that the Festival soon took on a life of its own, bursting out of the distilleries and on to the streets of the region's towns and villages.

There are, naturally, many whisky-related events such as tastings (including a whisky and chocolate tasting at Gordon & MacPhail's in Elgin), the Spirit of Speyside Malt Whisky Festival features: tastings, master classes in blending, the Dufftown Distilleries Walk, the Colours of Whisky art exhibition, and a train tour of suitably located distilleries.

master classes in blending, the Dufftown Distilleries Walk, the Colours of Whisky art exhibition, and a train tour of suitably located distilleries. But it's not only whisky that's on show: Nature trails and wildlife walks, art and photography exhibitions (not necessarily whisky-related), the finest of Highland food and produce, pipe bands, an inter-village Topical Tattie-Bogle competition (that's scarecrows south of the Border)—every treasure that the region has to offer is laid out proudly. And because malt whisky and motoring don't mix all these events are linked by sponsored public transport, with a Festival Rambler bus allowing unlimited rides for a flat fee and generous discounts on taxi-fares.

The main Festival has grown year by year, with events lined up in recent years hovering around 400 and visitor numbers approaching 30,000, and there's now also a smaller event held in September—the other "shoulder month"—and based in Dufftown.

Appendix II

The Whisky Regions of Scotland

The Scotch Whisky Association divides the country's whisky producers into five regions—Highlands & Islands, Lowlands, Campbeltown, Islay, and Speyside—that mean absolutely nothing at all. They have no official status as indicators of geographic origin, they carry out no administrative functions, and they have no bearing whatever on the character of the whiskies produced within them.

The fact that they vary wildly in size—Lowlands and Campbeltown have three malt distilleries each, while Speyside has close to 50—is an indicator that these regions are purely historic and are in truth almost less artificial. Unlike the wine-growing districts of France, Italy, or Spain, no Scottish region has a characteristic soil or a distinctive climate or a native variety of barley. They date back, in fact, to the Wash Act of 1784, when in an attempt to curb illegal distilling, legislators drew an almost arbitrary line across a map to divide Highlands from Lowlands. The large, commercial, and in most cases law-abiding enterprises of the Lowlands paid full price for their licenses to distill, while the smaller distillers of the more rugged Highlands got a considerable concession but were not allowed to sell their whisky outside their own region. Somehow the concept of regionality survived the abolition of this ridiculous trade barrier in 1823, even though the geography of Scotland doesn't lend itself to the idea; and in due course more regions came along. There are now four, five, or six, depending on whether you count Speyside and The Islands as separate regions or not.

But the great definers of a whisky are whether it is derived from pure barley malt or mixed malted and unmalted grains of various cereals; how and with what fuel the barley has been malted; what kind of still has been used—pot or continuous—and the unique characteristics of that still; the mineral content of the water used both in mashing and in bottling; the way in which the stillman chooses to operate the equipment; and the preferred oaking regime. All these variables are peculiar to each individual distillery. You might be able to identify two wines as Burgundies, say, or Riojas, thanks to their shared regional origin; but unless you already knew, you'd never guess that Laphroaig and Bunnahabhain both came from Islay. Not only is the character of each whisky not determined by its region of origin, but more: Its region of origin (as opposed to its place of origin) has no discernible effect on the outcome whatever. It all comes down to the enormously variable ingredients and processes used in its manufacture; and, praise the lord, every whisky distillery has its own.

Appendix III

Distilleries Closed to the Public

O r are they? Their websites say they have no facilities and don't do tours; but Scotch whisky distillers are inordinately (and justifiably) proud of what they do and simply can't resist sharing if they get the chance. So if there's a particular distillery you've always been burning to tour, ring and ask. The worst they can do is snarl some terrifying Gaelic swear-word down the phone at you. A tip: It will help if there is a small group of you. Another tip: It will help even more if you are (or can make a convincing case that you are) the Duluth Chapter of the Whisky Lovers of America or the Chesterfield & Staveley Malt Maniacs or some such.

Ailsa Bay   Grangestone Ind Est, Girvan KA26 9PT. 01465 713091

Allt-a-Bhainne   Glenrinnes AB55 4DB. 01542 783200

Arbikie Estate   Inverkeilor, Arbroath, Angus DD11 4UZ. 01241 830770

Auchroisk   Mulben AB55 6XS. 01466 795650

Aultmore   Keith AB55 6QY. 01542 881800

Balmenach   Cromdale, Grantown-on-Spey. 26 3PF. 01479 872569

Benrinnes   Aberlour AB38 9NN. 01340 871215

Braeval   Chapeltown, Ballindalloch AB37 9JS. 01542 783042

Craigellachie   Hill Street, Craigellachie AB38 9ST. 01340 872971

Dailuaine   Carron AB38 7RE. 01340 810361

Dalmunach   Carron AB38 7QP

Dufftown   Church Street, Dufftown AB55 4BR. 01340 822960

Glen Elgin   Longmorn, Elgin IV30 8SL. 01343 862100

Glen Spey   Rothes AB38 7AY. 01340 832000

Glenallachie   Glenallachie, Aberlour AB38 9LR. 01340 810361

Glenburgie   Alves, Forres IV36 2QY. 01343 554120

Glendullan   Low Road, Dufftown AB55 4DJ. 01340 822303

Glenlossie   Glenlossie Road, Thornshill, Elgin IV30 8SS.
01343 862000

Glenrothes   Rothes, Moray AB38 7AA. 01340 872300

Glentauchers   Mulben AB55 6YL. 01542 860272

Inchgower   Buckie AB56 5AB. 01542 836700

Knockando   Knockando AB38 7RT. 01479 874660

Linkwood   Linkwood Road, Elgin IV30 8RD. 01343 547004

Loch Lomond   Lomond Ind Est, Alexandria G83 0TL.
01389 752781

Longmorn   Lithe Lochan, Elgin IV30 8SJ. 01343 554120

Macduff   Banff AB45 3JT. 01261 812612

Miltonduff   Miltonduff, Elgin IV30 8TQ. 01343 554120

Mortlach   Fife Street, Dufftown AB55 4AQ. 01340 822100

Roseisle   Roseisle, Elgin IV30 5YP. 01343 832106

Speyside   Tromie Mills, Glentromie PH12 1NS. 01540 661060

Strathmill   Union Street, Keith AB55 5DQ. 01542 882295

Tamdhu   Knockando AB38 7RP. 01340 810695

Tamnavulin   Tomnavoulin AB37 9JA. 01479 818031

Teaninich   Riverside Drive, Alness IV17 0XB. 01349 885001

Tormore   Advie PH26 3LR. 01807 510244

Wolfburn   Henderson Park, Thurso KW14 7XW

APPENDIX IV
Distilleries Pending

The pace of new whisky distillery openings shows no sign of slowing down, with (at time of going to print) four due to open in 2017 and at least another three in various stages of completion. What no-one can know, of course, is how many others are on the drawing board, and how many more still are trembling in the moment of possibility between pipe dream and plan. But here, anyway, are some treats for the whisky tourist to look forward to.

■ Barra
Borve, Isle of Barra HS9 5XR

Having been in the pipeline since 2005, Isle of Barra's gestation period has been the longest since Speyside, which took 24 years from conception to the first new make. This bold plan for a completely sustainable distillery (own loch, own wind-generated electricity, own barley, own maltings) should finally come to fruition in 2019, helping generate tourism and revive crofting for the 35-square mile island at the extreme southern tip of the Outer Hebrides and its mainly Gaelic-speaking 1,300 people.

■ Clydeside
Queen's Dock, Glasgow
theclydeside.com

This £10 million project led by Tim Morrison, current scion of the dynasty that until 1994 owned Bowmore, Auchentoshan, and Glen Garioch, to revive distilling in the very heart of Glasgow should make Queen's Dock the city's busiest tourist hotspot. It already boasts such attractions as the enormous Finnieston Crane, the preserved barque the Glenlee, the new Riverside Museum, and the Hydro Arena among others. Clydeside Distillery, which is due to open in mid-2017, occupies the former pumphouse built by Tim's great-grandfather in 1877 and will include a shop, cafe, whisky museum and tasting rooms. Consult the website for up-to-date visitor information.

■ *Drimnin*

Drimnin Estate, Lochaline, Morvern, Argyll PA80 5XZ.
07714 248425. enquiries@drimninestate.co.uk

Sandwiched between the Ardnamurchan Peninsula with its new distillery to the north and the Isle of Mull, home to the Tobermory Distillery, to the south is the rugged and astonishingly beautiful Morvern Peninsula where you will find the 7,000-acre Drimnin Estate and its new distillery. Built in 1850, Drimnin House is a splendid example of a Victorian Gothic mansion, but by 2002 when the current owners bought it, both the house and the estate were sadly decayed. A rolling program of restoration since then has concentrated on farming and outdoor activities, with guest accommodation in the house itself and the many and various estate cottages. The crowning glory of all this is a small malt distillery sited in the outbuildings of the old home farm, which should be open for visitors by Easter 2017, all going well. And when it does open, it will just pip Ardnamurchan's claim to being the most westerly distillery on the British mainland.

■ *Falkirk*

The Helix Project, Falkirk FK2. 01324 670000
info@falkirkdistillery.com

Bringing distilling back to Falkirk since the much-lamented closure of Rosebank in 1993, the Falkirk Distillery is part of a £25 million complex of shops, restaurants, and conference facilities which is in itself part of the £43 million regeneration of the eastern side of this historic town. Ground was broken at the site as long ago as 2010, and it should finally be open to the public in early 2017. It has its own visitor center which the developers behind the Helix Project believe will attract some 75,000 tourists a year, and it's also part of a grand plan for a tourist trail linking it with the famous Kelpies statues in Helix Park, the palatial Callendar House in its landscaped grounds, and the astonishing Falkirk Wheel boat lift on the canal junction just to the west of town. Much of the distillery equipment at Falkirk comes from Caperdonich in Rothes on Speyside, which closed in 2002. It's hoped, though, that the finished whisky will be a light, aromatic floral Lowlander just as Rosebank was.

■ *Gartbreck*

Moss Road, Bowmore, Islay PA43 7JG. 01496 511301

When and whether Islay's ninth distillery is going to appear is still something of a mystery. Jean Donnay, founder of Brittany's Glann Ar Mor distillery, obtained planning permission to convert Gartbreck Farm, a stone's throw from Bowmore, into a new malt distillery in 2014 and originally planned to open in late 2015. At the time, though Glann Ar Mor was going through a bad patch of its own and work on the Gartbreck site was postponed. Hopefully progress can be resumed since Gartbreck promises to be a rarity, using direct-fired stills and an old-fashioned worm-tub just as Glann Ar Mor does.

■ *Lindores*

Lindores Abbey Farm, Abbey Road, Newburgh, Fife.

This is sacred ground for whisky lovers, for it was the home of Brother John Cor, the Benedictine monk to whom in June 1495 King James IV of Scotland granted eight bolls (or nearly 1,700 liters dry measure) of malt "ad faciendum aquavite"—to make aqua vitae. This probably didn't mean whisky but rather a neutral alcohol in which medicinal herbs would be steeped to dissolve their alkaloid active components, and therefore more similar to gin. But it's the very first mention in Britain of the use of malt liquor rather than wine in distillation. Anyway, a derelict farmstead next to the ruins of Lindores Abbey is shortly to be the home of the first distillery on the site since 1559, when the abbey was forcibly closed during the Scottish reformation. Andrew McKenzie Smith, whose family has owned the land for more than a century, submitted plans in May 2015 for a distillery and visitor center, and when the complex eventually opens it will doubtless become a place of pilgrimage for whisky lovers from all over the world.

■ *Raasay & Borders*

23 Manor Place, Edinburgh EH3 7DX. 0131 564 0761

An ambitious project to create not one craft distillery but two—one on the tiny island of Raasay (population 161) off the east coast of Skye, the other in an as-yet unspecified location in the Borders region—should start to bear fruit in mid-2017, all going well. The venture is the brainchild of businessman Bill Dobbie and food industry executive Alistair Day, whose great-grandfather was a whisky blender in Coldstream and whose 100-year-old cellar-book inspired Alistair to create the Tweedale super-premium blend, which in turn led to the creation of R&B. Raasay Distillery along with a visitor center and eight letting rooms was granted planning permission in February 2016: It will occupy Borodale House, an 1870s villa which was for a long while a hotel and then briefly the Raasay Outdoor Centre before R&B bought it in 2013. Meanwhile the partners are still looking for the ideal site for the Borders half of the enterprise.

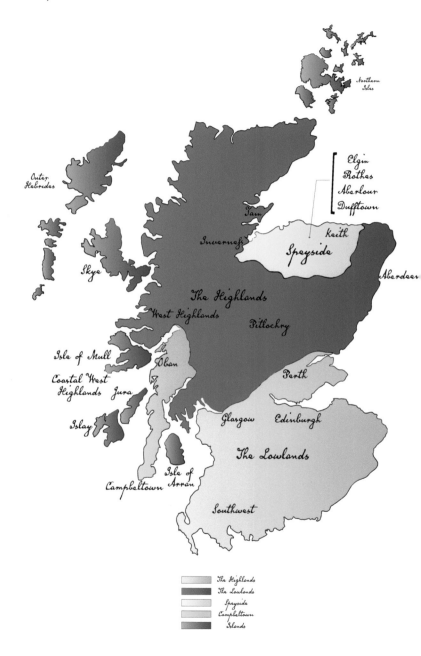

CPSIA information can be obtained
at www.ICGtesting.com
Printed in the USA
LVHW02n2358080318
569225LV00001B/2/P